# The SportingNews SELECTS

# LEGENDS of COLLEGE BASKETBALL

BY
MIKE DeCOURCY

R=Right  L=Left  T=Top  B=Bottom  M=Middle

**Front Cover:** Rich Clarkson & Associates *(clockwise from top center)* Lew Alcindor, Isiah Thomas, Pete Maravich, Magic Johnson, Michael Jordan, Patrick Ewing, Bill Walton.

**Back Cover:** Rich Clarkson & Associates

**AllSport:** 126, 127, 166, 167

**AP/Wide World Photos:** 9TL, 36, 48, 58, 59, 64, 65, 88, 93, 96, 98, 122, 123, 124, 129, 134, 139, 140, 141, 142, 143, 146, 152, 154, 155, 174, 175, 178, 180, 181, 186, 188, 189

**Rich Clarkson:** 2, 3, 4, 5, 9R, 10L, 11, 12, 13, 14, 15, 16, 17, 18, 20, 21, 22, 23, 24, 25, 26, 27, 29, 30, 32, 33, 34, 35, 37, 38, 39, 40, 41, 42, 43, 46, 47, 49, 52, 53, 54, 55, 56, 57, 66, 69, 72, 73, 74, 75, 78, 79, 86, 87, 89, 90, 91, 100, 101, 106, 107, 110, 111, 112, 113, 115, 118, 125, 128, 130, 131, 137, 147, 149, 156, 160, 161, 164, 165, 172, 173, 176, 177, 185, 190, 191

**The Courier-Journal:** 92

**The Sporting News Archives:** 6,7, 9BL, 19, 28, 44, 45, 50, 51, 60, 61, 62, 67, 68, 76, 77, 80, 81, 94, 95, 99, 102, 103, 119, 132, 148, 157, 170, 171, 184, 192

**Malcolm Emmons:** 10R, 63, 70, 71, 84, 85, 104, 105, 114, 116, 117, 135, 136, 138

**Bruce L. Schwartzman:** 120, 121

**Courtesy of Bradley University Instructional Technology and Production Services:** 179

**Courtesy of LaSalle University:** 150, 151

**Courtesy of University of Louisiana at Lafayette:** 153

**Courtesy of University of Maryland Athletic Media Relations:** 168, 169

**Courtesy of University of Massachusetts Media Relations:** 162, 163

**Courtesy of Niagara University:** 97

**Courtesy of University of North Carolina:** 187

**Courtesy of Wake Forest University Media Relations:** 182, 183

**Bob Leverone/The Sporting News:** 82, 83, 108, 109, 158, 159

**Ohio State University:** 31

**Robert Seale/The Sporting News:** 133, 144, 145

# Photo Credits

# Acknowledgements

Without question, Mike DeCourcy is one of the finest basketball writers I know. From a journalist's perspective, Mike is an outstanding reporter and an outstanding writer, and the combination of those skills brings readers information and analysis on college basketball each and every week in THE SPORTING NEWS, and in this book. What sets Mike apart from his counterparts, too, is his absolute unbridled passion and enthusiasm for the game. This is a guy who does college basketball year-round, in-season and out-of-season, who vacations at summer basketball camps.

When we began this project, there could be no better person to provide the historical context and information, and ranking, than Mike DeCourcy. Many thanks to him for his dedication to this project.

When it came time to putting the words and pictures together, Bob Parajon's design team led by Matt Kindt and including Dave Brickey, Steve Romer, Pamela Speh and Vern Kasal created a beautiful package. What they did is accomplish an attractive design that provides the pertinent basic information with the text and images that let you know those special qualities about the 100 players featured in this book.

Steve Meyerhoff
Executive Editor

The Sporting News SELECTS

# LEGENDS OF COLLEGE BASKETBALL

The Sporting News

SELECTS LEGENDS C0

LLEGE BASKETBALL

# Introduction

The first college basketball game was played in 1895 featuring nine-man teams from Minnesota A&M and Hamline College. Or it was contested in 1896 when a five-man team from the University of Iowa faced the Chicago YMCA. Or it might have been 1897, when Yale and Penn opposed each other and both sides had five genuine college men. The dispute over the origins of college basketball is not one that has raged ferociously during the past century, but it does show that even from the start its fans have savored a good argument.

Unlike its brother sport of college football, basketball prefers to settle its championship on the field of play rather than by vote and debate. Of course, there still is plenty to discuss, principally the selection and seeding of the teams that will compose the NCAA Tournament field.

And, as much as anything, basketball fans love to quarrel about players. Magic or Bird? Wilt or Russell? Walton or Alcindor? The great players, the Legends of College Basketball, are one constant through the sport's persistent change.

No American sports entity has been altered as rapidly and thoroughly in the past three decades. In 1975, there were 10 major-college players on the NBA draft's early entry list. Dunking was not permitted. The NCAA championship game was played before an audience of 15,151. The tournament field included 32 teams.

Now, the college game is ruled by the 3-point field goal, the 35-second shot clock and the departure of star players to the NBA Draft. The tournament field features 64 teams. The Final Four draws more than 40,000 spectators.

Great players helped drive college basketball's growth in popularity—so many there was not room to acknowledge all on a list of the sport's 100 best. Among the missing: Wake Forest center Dickie Hemric, Holy Cross forward Tom Heinsohn, Seton Hall center Walter Dukes, Tennessee forward Bernard King, Michigan forward Glen Rice and Duke forward Grant Hill. Given the commitment so many players made to the game, one important prerequisite was established. Those who played only through their sophomore seasons and did not win national championships were not welcome.

Because of the enduring genius of coaches Adolph Rupp and Dean Smith—and the depth of talent they attracted and developed—Kentucky and North Carolina have two of the richest NCAA basketball heritages. However, neither program had a player ranked in the top 15. Each easily could have had another three players in the top 100, if there were room: Kentucky's Cotton Nash, Bill Spivey and Jamal Mashburn might have elbowed their way in, and the same with North Carolina's Charlie Scott, Larry Miller and Sam Perkins.

A fundamental oddity has remained through the sport's history: many of the best teams do not feature the greatest players, but the greatest players always make their teams better.

**Clockwise from top left: Bernard King, Grant Hill, Walter Dukes**

# The Players

# 1 Lew ALCINDOR

Near the start of Lew Alcindor's playing career at UCLA, coach John Wooden called him aside for a little chat about the goals he might pursue during his three years in the Bruins' lineup. Wooden presented a scenario in which Alcindor would be passed the ball as often as possible and could shoot as much as he liked.

"We could have made him the highest scorer in collegiate history," Wooden said. "He said he didn't want to do that. And I knew that, or I wouldn't have mentioned it."

Alcindor scored plenty for the Bruins during his three seasons. His 26.4 scoring average is the highest for any player in the program's rich history. He scored a school-record 61 points in a 1967 Pacific-8 Conference game against Washington State. This mattered little compared to what he and his Bruins teammates accomplished as the 1960s stormed to a close and college basketball surged in popularity among the nation's sports fans.

During Alcindor's three seasons, the Bruins compiled an 88-2 record, including 41-1 in the Pac-8 and 12-0 in NCAA Tournament games that imparted three national championships. Alcindor was named Most Outstanding Player in three consecutive tournaments, the only player so honored.

Standing 7-2 gave him enough of an advantage, but he had athletic gifts to enhance that edge. "In comparison with other post men, he was quicker," Wooden said. "That's what I wanted in my players more than anything else."

Because of his size, it was easy for Alcindor to score on dunks. That was gone following his first season at UCLA, banned by rules makers in a move interpreted as a reaction to his superiority. Wooden said it was best for Alcindor, encouraging him to develop his shooting and the awesome "sky hook."

Alcindor had a reliable hook shot when he arrived at UCLA, but Wooden wanted him to modify the technique to remove the sweeping arm motion. He preferred Alcindor extend his arm and cut loose the ball with a flick of the wrist. This became basketball's only indefensible weapon. It helped Alcindor, who took the name Kareem Abdul-Jabbar after converting to Islam, score 38,387 points in the National Basketball Association. No one ever scored more.

**Born: April 16, 1947, New York**

*"We could have made him the highest scorer in collegiate history. He said he didn't want to do that. And I knew that, or I wouldn't have mentioned it."*

—John Wooden

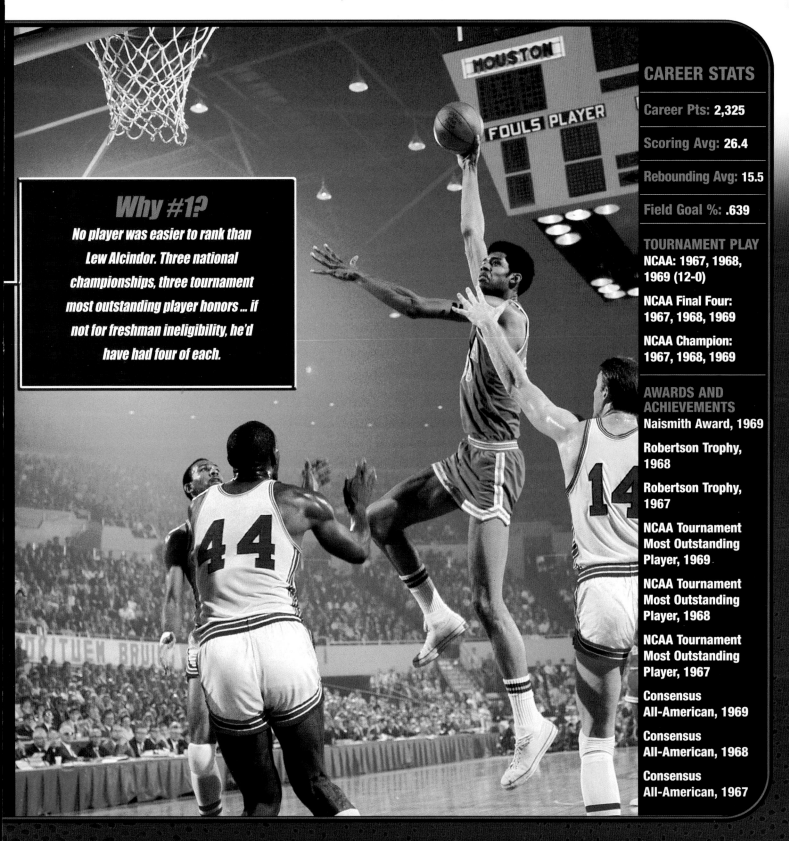

### Why #1?

*No player was easier to rank than Lew Alcindor. Three national championships, three tournament most outstanding player honors ... if not for freshman ineligibility, he'd have had four of each.*

## CAREER STATS

Career Pts: **2,325**

Scoring Avg: **26.4**

Rebounding Avg: **15.5**

Field Goal %: **.639**

### TOURNAMENT PLAY
NCAA: 1967, 1968, 1969 (12-0)

NCAA Final Four: 1967, 1968, 1969

NCAA Champion: 1967, 1968, 1969

### AWARDS AND ACHIEVEMENTS
Naismith Award, 1969

Robertson Trophy, 1968

Robertson Trophy, 1967

NCAA Tournament Most Outstanding Player, 1969

NCAA Tournament Most Outstanding Player, 1968

NCAA Tournament Most Outstanding Player, 1967

Consensus All-American, 1969

Consensus All-American, 1968

Consensus All-American, 1967

**Height/Weight:** 7-2/240   **High School:** Power Memorial Academy, New York   **College:** UCLA, 1966-1969

# 2. BiLL WALTON

Bill Walton's brilliance was not the least bit about statistics. Yet it is impossible to ignore the sequence of numbers that profoundly illustrates his supremacy over his fellow collegians: 21-of-22. Few fans do not recognize the significance of those figures.

In the 1973 NCAA championship in St. Louis, Walton attempted 22 shots and made 21 for a 44-point night that destroyed Memphis State and still stands as a title-game record. That did not represent spectacular shooting. Many of those baskets required Walton simply to drop the ball into the goal. His quickness and intelligence were such he gained position on the Tigers defenders at will.

"I got a lot of individual credit, but that night was really John Wooden and UCLA basketball at its best," Walton said. "The ball movement and execution were perfect. It was the team flow, the team movement—and Coach Wooden's insistence the ball keep coming in until they stopped it."

The 1973 championship was the second of two UCLA won with Walton, but nearly three decades later he still was bothered by the one that got away—to North Carolina State in 1974, the only interruption in a string of Bruins titles from 1967 to 1975. "As Coach Wooden told us," Walton said, "when you beat yourself you'll never get over it."

At UCLA, Walton's boundless athleticism allowed him to leap high above the rim for blocks and rebounds. The elevation on his unusual jump shot—hands cupped beneath the ball, elbows nearly touching below—made it difficult to challenge. His ability to pass made the Bruins a chore to defend. "He was tremendous at making the outlet pass to get our fastbreak going," Wooden said. "He seemed to know instinctively where to find the man."

Walton developed his skills as a skinny teenaged guard who later grew into a center's body. He saw his first televised game at age 12, when UCLA defeated Michigan in the 1965 title game. Gail Goodrich set the championship record with 42 points in the Bruins' victory. Transfixed by what he saw, Walton vowed to play at UCLA and break that mark. The numbers from that night will remain with him always.

*Born: Nov. 5, 1952, La Mesa, Calif.*

*"He was tremendous at making the outlet pass to get our fastbreak going. He seemed to know instinctively where to find the man."*

—John Wooden

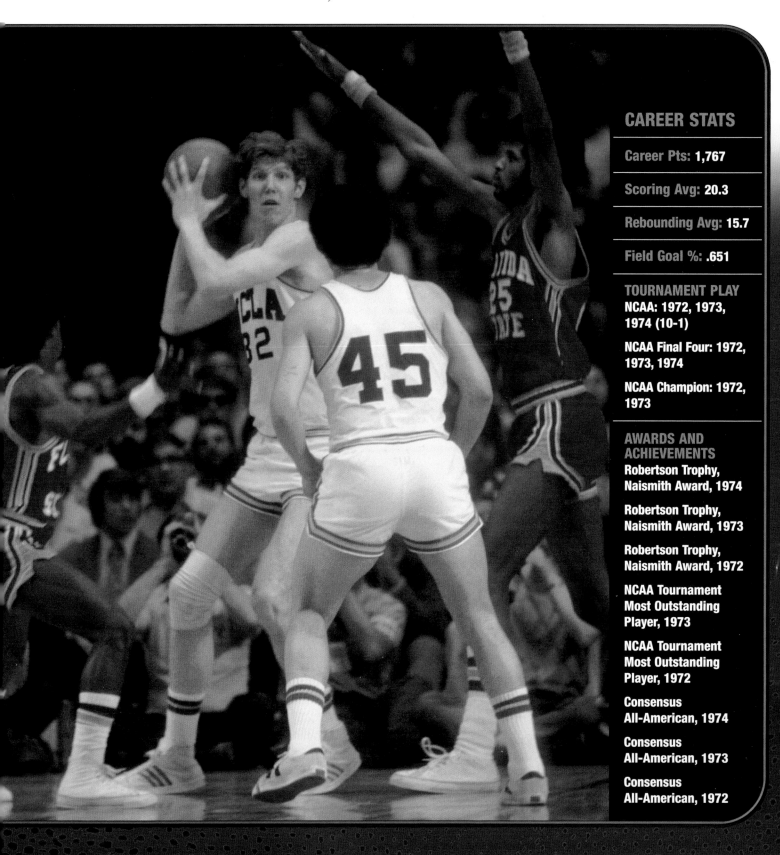

## CAREER STATS

**Career Pts: 1,767**

**Scoring Avg: 20.3**

**Rebounding Avg: 15.7**

**Field Goal %: .651**

### TOURNAMENT PLAY
**NCAA: 1972, 1973, 1974 (10-1)**

**NCAA Final Four: 1972, 1973, 1974**

**NCAA Champion: 1972, 1973**

### AWARDS AND ACHIEVEMENTS
**Robertson Trophy, Naismith Award, 1974**

**Robertson Trophy, Naismith Award, 1973**

**Robertson Trophy, Naismith Award, 1972**

**NCAA Tournament Most Outstanding Player, 1973**

**NCAA Tournament Most Outstanding Player, 1972**

**Consensus All-American, 1974**

**Consensus All-American, 1973**

**Consensus All-American, 1972**

*Height/Weight: 6-11/230    High School: Helix High, La Mesa    College: UCLA, 1971-1974*

# 3 Oscar ROBERTSON

## CAREER STATS

**Career Pts: 2,973**

**Scoring Avg: 33.8**

**Rebounding Avg: 15.2**

**Field Goal %: .535**

### TOURNAMENT PLAY
**NCAA: 1958, 1959, 1960 (4-3)**

**NCAA Final Four: 1959, 1960**

### AWARDS AND ACHIEVEMENTS
**U.S. Basketball Writers Player of the Year, 1960**

**U.S. Basketball Writers Player of the Year, 1959**

**The Sporting News Player of the Year, 1958**

**Consensus All-American, 1960**

**Consensus All-American, 1959**

**Consensus All-American, 1958**

*Born: Nov. 24, 1938, Charlotte, Tenn.*

## He had a power forward's strength, a small forward's agility, a shooting guard's touch and the passing to match the very best point guard. He had a coach's ability to think and lead.

No player mastered as many elements of basketball as Oscar Robertson. The game's primary measures are points, rebounds and assists, and Robertson had each of them covered. He had a power forward's strength, a small forward's agility, a shooting guard's touch and the passing to match the very best point guard. He had a coach's ability to think and lead.

Robertson topped the nation in scoring as a sophomore, averaging 35.1 points and besting the 50-point mark four times. He again was No. 1 as a junior and senior and was more than two points better than his closest challenger all three years. Robertson collected more than 15 rebounds per game. Combining his 7.1 assists with his scoring meant Robertson was responsible for 47 of the 85 points his team generated on an average night.

Cincinnati was not a basketball power before Robertson. The Bearcats never had been to the NCAA Tournament. And, somewhat to his surprise, they never had included a black player on their roster.

Indiana was just about everything Cincinnati was not, including Robertson's home-state school. The Hoosiers had won two NCAA titles under coach Branch McCracken. When Robertson met McCracken, however, he felt disrespected and unwelcome and vowed never to play for the Hoosiers. Robertson's decision to join the Bearcats helped the school establish the kind of program that led to five consecutive Final Four appearances and two national championships.

Though he bore considerable responsibility, Robertson did not get to experience those two titles. They came in 1961 and 1962, following his graduation. If Robertson had not become a Bearcat, it is unlikely George Wilson, Tom Thacker, Tony Yates and Paul Hogue would have enrolled. Cincinnati went from zero black players to four black starters in five years. Such was Robertson's allure, his strength as a pioneer.

Cincinnati made the Final Four twice with Robertson, but lost to California in the semifinals in 1959 and 1960. Coaching genius Pete Newell devised defensive schemes that slowed the pace and forced Robertson to shoot less frequently and from less advantageous positions. Newell's college teams had faced Bill Russell, Wilt Chamberlain, Elgin Baylor. However, in "A Good Man," the biography of Newell, the coach admitted, "We hadn't played against anyone as good as Oscar."

**Height/Weight:** 6-5/220   **High School:** Crispus Attucks High, Indianapolis   **College:** University of Cincinnati, 1957-1960

# 4 BILL RUSSELL

The game of basketball Bill Russell brought to San Francisco in 1953 bore only a passing resemblance to that which had been played during the first half of the 20th century. There still was a ball and a hoop, but Russell did more to prevent their introduction than any player before or since.

The sport was mostly about offense before Russell led USF to consecutive national championships in 1955 and 1956 and a 59-1 record those two years, but he showed what was possible if teams committed to affecting the game defensively.

"Defense is a science—not a helter-skelter thing you just luck into. Every move has six or seven years of work behind it," Russell said in the book, "Champion of American Sports." Phil Woolpert, the coach of the Dons, believed firmly in defensive basketball and found in Russell his prize student.

Russell's jumping and timing made him so effective as a shot-blocker that fans and opponents were forced to pay attention. Even if Russell was not affecting the game by scoring points—which he did more than is widely perceived—he could control the action by denying opponents effective access to the baseline and the lane.

Though Russell owned enough athletic talent to clear 6-9½ as a competitive high jumper at USF, he was not an immediate success in basketball. He served as a team mascot one year and did not excel until his senior season at McClymonds High in Oakland, Calif.

Russell did not grow to his full height until after arriving at USF. He learned to play the center position with the freshman team and immediately became a force when he joined the varsity as a sophomore, averaging 19.9 points and 19.2 rebounds. He is one of only six players with career averages of at least 20 points and 20 rebounds.

In the second week of the 1954-55 season, San Francisco lost a game to a top-20 UCLA team. The Dons did not lose again until after Russell departed, the winning streak eventually reaching 60 games. Russell never was about numbers, but the ones that mattered most always were healthy when he competed.

**Born: Feb. 12, 1934, Monroe, La.**

*Russell's jumping and timing made him so effective as a shot-blocker that fans and opponents were forced to pay attention.*

## CAREER STATS

Career Pts: **1,636**

Scoring Avg: **20.7**

Rebounding Avg: **20.3**

Field Goal %: **.516**

### TOURNAMENT PLAY
NCAA: **1955, 1956 (9-0)**

NCAA Champion: **1955, 1956**

### AWARDS AND ACHIEVEMENTS
United Press International Player of the Year, 1956

NCAA Tournament Most Outstanding Player, 1955

Consensus All-American, 1956

Consensus All-American, 1955

*Height/Weight:* **6-10/215**   *High School:* **McClymonds High, Oakland, Calif.**   *College:* **University of San Francisco, 1953-1956**

# 5 Pete MARAVICH

## CAREER STATS

**Career Pts: 3,667**

**Scoring Avg: 44.2**

**Assists: 5.1**

**Field Goal %: .438**

## TOURNAMENT PLAY
**NIT: 1970**

## AWARDS AND ACHIEVEMENTS
**Robertson Trophy, Naismith Award, 1970**

**Robertson Trophy, 1969**

**Consensus All-American, 1970**

**Consensus All-American, 1969**

**Consensus All-American, 1968**

*Born: June 22, 1947, Aliquippa, Pa.   Died: Jan. 5, 1988   Height/Weight: 6-5/200   High School: Broughton High, Raleigh, N.C.*

*"If I have a choice whether to do the show or throw a straight pass and we're going to get the basket either way, I'm going to do the show."*

—Pete Maravich

There wasn't a whole lot worth watching during LSU's 1966-67 season. The Tigers struggled to a mere three victories. However, for the price of admission to a home game at the Parker Agricultural Center, fans could see Pete Maravich play for the freshman team. So they showed up early and left when he was done.

Maravich rarely failed to entertain. NCAA basketball has not been home to a greater offensive weapon. With a ball in his hands, Maravich thrilled spectators and panicked defenders.

He could shoot from all distances, from all angles, with either hand, sometimes without looking at the target. He could make the ball appear to have stopped in mid-air, then slap it toward a teammate once the defense was frozen. He could put so much spin on a bounce-pass it would cut sideways and befuddle all but its target.

"If I have a choice whether to do the show or throw a straight pass and we're going to get the basket either way," Maravich once said, "I'm going to do the show."

Maravich overtook Oscar Robertson's NCAA career scoring record in January of his senior season. He needed 40 points in a home game against Ole Miss, and even Rebels coach Cob Jarvis admitted the mark would fall. Maravich scored 53 in a Tigers victory, and continued on until he'd scored 694 points more than the Big O.

However, Maravich's circumstance at LSU was complicated by the fact he was coached by his father, Press. It became common to suggest he was problematic as a teammate, by way of explaining why he did not play for championship teams. He dominated the ball, certainly, but shared it enough to average 6.2 assists as a senior, when his teammates improved enough to take advantage of his passes.

The Tigers were only two games over .500 his first two seasons, but that represented a huge improvement. As a senior, he carried them to a 22-10 season and fourth-place finish in the NIT. He ignited a taste for the game that led LSU to become an SEC power during the next two decades. He was more than a showman, but as a showman he had no peer.

*College: Louisiana State U., 1967-1970*

# 6 David THOMPSON

## CAREER STATS

**Career Pts: 2,309**

**Scoring Avg: 26.8**

**Rebounding Avg: 8.1**

**Field Goal %: .553**

## TOURNAMENT PLAY
**NCAA: 1974 (4-0)**

**NCAA Final Four: 1974**

**NCAA Champion: 1974**

## AWARDS AND ACHIEVEMENTS
**Robertson Trophy, Naismith Award, 1975**

**Associated Press Player of the Year, 1974**

**NCAA Tournament Most Outstanding Player, 1974**

**Consensus All-American, 1975**

**Consensus All-American, 1974**

**Consensus All-American, 1973**

*Born: July 13, 1954 , Boiling Springs, N.C.*

> *"The alley-oop was a spectacular play, and it showed a lot of finesse and body-control, but it would have been a lot easier to catch it and dunk it."*
>
> — David Thompson

David Thompson thought he'd been fouled attempting a jump shot. He was not pleased. It was time, he figured, to show the Pittsburgh Panthers something special, some play that would shake the foundation of their confidence. So Thompson jetted to seize a defensive rebound as it bounced high above the rim.

Unfortunately, he tripped on a teammate's shoulder.

Thompson, the highest-flying All-American ever, caught his instep on 6-5 forward Phil Spence and tumbled headfirst to the court. It was a terrifying fall. He was done for the day, but his teammates broke away for an easy victory in the 1974 NCAA Tournament East Region final. It wasn't just an ordinary game-ending injury, though. The incident was a declaration that anything was possible with Thompson.

That included an interruption of the UCLA dynasty, which Thompson occasioned with 28 points in a double-overtime comeback victory over the Bruins in the national semifinals. He scored another 21 as Marquette fell in the NCAA title game.

He had a shooting guard's body, but he jumped so high it made sense to play him at forward, where he could affect the game in unpredictable ways. Thompson was an excellent jump shooter, but he was most dangerous floating near the rim, tipping balls into the goal or catching "alley-oop" lob passes from point guard Monte Towe and—given the no-dunk rule—dropping them through the net.

"I was pretty proficient at dropping it in," Thompson said. "The alley-oop was a spectacular play, and it showed a lot of finesse and body-control, but it would have been a lot easier to catch it and dunk it."

Thompson was named Atlantic Coast Conference player of the year in all three of his seasons. N.C. State compiled a 79-7 record that included a 27-0 mark his sophomore year, when the Pack was ineligible for the NCAA Tournament. They were 24-0 in the ACC in 1973 and 1974.

"To do that, we would have to be considered one of the best teams of all time," Thompson said. "The ACC always had three teams ranked in the top 5 or 10—it was a very tough conference." With David Thompson on the roster—and in the air—anything seemed possible.

**Height/Weight:** 6-4/195    **High School:** Crest (N.C.) High    **College:** North Carolina State University, 1972-1975

# 7 Elvin HAYES

The court was placed at the center of the Astrodome, so far from the seats that nearly everyone under that famous roof had an equally dreadful seat for Houston vs. UCLA—or was it Elvin Hayes vs. Lew Alcindor? When the game began, there was no doubt what was happening. Hayes was the best player on the floor on that night, the night that revolutionized college basketball.

A 6-9 forward, Hayes scored 39 points, grabbed 15 rebounds and blocked eight shots. Alcindor settled for 15 points, 12 rebounds and a 71-69 defeat that was one of only two he experienced as a Bruin. The nationally televised game helped make college basketball a sport for the masses. The result helped make Hayes, The Big E, a household name.

As a high school player, he was not well known even to college recruiters. When Hayes grew up in Rayville, La., the town was painfully segregated. He played basketball at the only place where a black teenager was allowed, the gym at Eula D. Britton High.

It was different at Houston. The year Hayes graduated from high school, the university chose to integrate its athletic program. The Cougars staff was tipped off regarding Hayes' potential by a coach from Texas Southern, a historically black college in Houston. Hayes became one of the greatest recruiting "sleepers."

A center his first season, Hayes averaged 27.2 points and 16.9 rebounds for a 23-6 team. When the Cougars added 6-8 Melvin Bell the following year, Hayes somewhat reluctantly moved to power forward. It was the position he was born to play. He developed a baseline turnaround jumper as unstoppable as Alcindor's sky hook. In his last two seasons, Houston went 58-6 and Hayes scored 2,095 points and grabbed 1,112 rebounds. Those years alone would represent a phenomenal career for any player.

However, in the 1968 Final Four, a rematch of the Astrodome game ended with Hayes scoring 10 points and UCLA winning. Hayes chose not to focus on the Bruins' revenge.

"UCLA won many big games, but they had lost one of the most historical games in basketball," he later told the *Dallas Morning News.* "The whole world remembers."

**Born: Nov. 17, 1945, Rayville, La.**

*Hayes was the best player on the floor on that night, the night that revolutionized college basketball.*

## CAREER STATS

Career Pts: **2,884**

Scoring Avg: **31.0**

Rebounding Avg: **17.2**

Field Goal %: **.536**

TOURNAMENT PLAY
**NCAA: 1966, 1967, 1968 (7-3)**

**NCAA Final Four: 1967, 1968**

AWARDS AND ACHIEVEMENTS
**Associated Press Player of the Year, 1968**

**Consensus All-American, 1968**

**Consensus All-American, 1967**

*Height/Weight: 6-9/230    High School: Eula D. Britton High, Rayville    College: University of Houston, 1965-1968*

# 8 Larry BIRD

There were so many skeptics, and many were difficult to dismiss. Billy Packer was a prominent network television broadcaster. He openly argued Indiana State did not warrant a No. 1 ranking in 1978-79 because its opposition was not challenging. The Sycamores charged unbeaten through 29 games entering the NCAA Tournament, but they competed in the Missouri Valley Conference. How could they possibly rank with the nation's best?

Larry Bird answered that question himself, though he preferred to do so by playing. He was by far the most publicized player that season and earned every major player of the year award, but he tried to elude the journalists eager to acquaint the public with his story. When he showed up as required at the news conference prior to the 1979 NCAA championship game, he surprised the assembled reporters by responding to questions he'd dodged all winter. One asked why he'd suddenly changed his policy. Bird's response: "You don't think I'm enjoying this, do you?"

Bird was happiest in a small town, playing basketball with minimal distractions. As a teenager, he was uncomfortable enough in crowds that he left Indiana University's busy campus after less than a month, robbing Bob Knight of the chance to coach one of the game's greatest players. Indiana State seemed more Bird's speed, but he soon had the basketball program moving in a direction that could not have been imagined.

Bird had unlimited range as a shooter and an unfathomable touch. He was one of the most instinctive passers the game has seen. His size and amazing hands made him a voracious rebounder. In three seasons at Indiana State, his teams averaged 27 victories.

The Sycamores made the NCAA once, entering 1979 as the No. 1 seed in the Midwest Region. A senior, Bird led the Sycamores past Virginia Tech, Oklahoma, Arkansas and DePaul, averaging 29.3 points, 13.5 rebounds and 5.5 assists. There was no doubting the competition nor Bird's ability. Michigan State and Magic Johnson ultimately stopped Indiana State in the title game with a 2-3 matchup zone that surrounded Bird on every touch. He shot 7-of-21 from the field. So Indiana State was not No. 1. It was No. 2, but had proved its point.

*Born: Dec. 7, 1956, West Baden, Ind.*

*Bird had unlimited range as a shooter and an unfathomable touch.*
*He was one of the most instinctive passers the game has seen. His size*
*and amazing hands made him a voracious rebounder.*

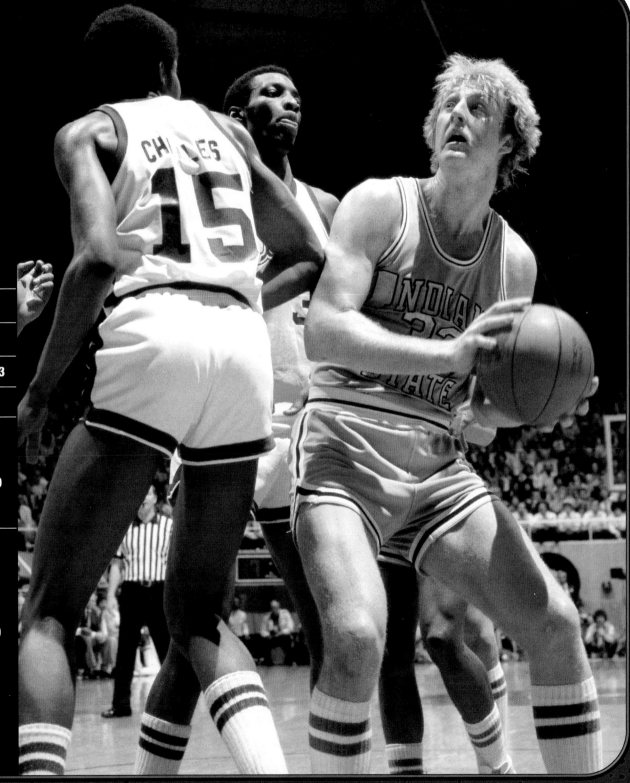

## CAREER STATS

**Career Pts: 2,850**

**Scoring Avg: 30.3**

**Rebounding Avg: 13.3**

**Field Goal %: .533**

### TOURNAMENT PLAY
**NCAA: 1979 (4-1)**

**NCAA Final Four: 1979**

**NIT: 1978**

### AWARDS AND ACHIEVEMENTS
**Robertson Trophy, 1979**

**Naismith Award, 1979**

**Wooden Award, 1979**

**Consensus All-American, 1979**

**Consensus All-American, 1978**

*Height/Weight:* **6-9/220**   *High School:* **Springs Valley High, French Lick, Ind.**   *College:* **Indiana State University, 1976-1979**

# 9 Christian LAETTNER

## Why #9?

*Although Christian Laettner did not achieve the same pro stardom as many at the top of this list, he was the greatest player in the history of the NCAA Tournament and the college game's best pressure player.*

It was supposed to be Alonzo Mourning's day. He had been the nation's preeminent freshman, leading Georgetown to a 29-4 record and the 1989 East Region final. That game instead revealed Duke's Christian Laettner as the dominant college player for the next four years.

Expected to be a backup as the year began, then gradually winning a starting job, his brilliance remained a secret before he led the Blue Devils past Georgetown. Laettner grabbed nine rebounds, scored 24 points on 9-of-10 shooting and began his ascent toward status as the greatest player in the history of the NCAA Tournament.

Laettner scored more points and played in more games than anyone in the event's history. He is the only player to start on four Final Four teams. He twice made game-ending, buzzer-beating shots in regional finals. He was the leading scorer on 1991 and 1992 teams that became the first since the end of the UCLA dynasty to repeat as NCAA champion.

"Christian wanted us to be great," said Mike Krzyzewski, Laettner's coach at Duke. "He had the ability to believe at the highest level."

Laettner could be a prickly sort whose demands for excellence sometimes irritated teammates. Krzyzewski compared him to a fire; the person in charge can use it to heat a building, or the fire can escape his control and consume the entire structure. Most often, opponents got burned.

In the 1991 Final Four, Laettner scored 28 points and made two crucial free throws to carry the Blue Devils past undefeated UNLV in the semifinals. They defeated Kansas in the championship game and claimed the school's first NCAA title.

As a senior, Laettner delivered his most memorable performance: 10-of-10 from the field and 10-of-10 from the free-throw line in the 1992 East Regional final against Kentucky. That included an 18-foot jumper off a long pass from forward Grant Hill with 2.1 seconds left, a shot that made the Blue Devils 104-103 winners in what is widely considered the greatest college game.

"He hit more big shots. He loved playing on the road. He took the ridicule of everyone," Krzyzewski said. "He's as good a winner as there was in college basketball."

*Born: August 17, 1969 , Angola, N.Y.*

> "He hit more big shots. He loved playing on the road. He took the ridicule of everyone. He's as good a winner as there was in college basketball."
> — Mike Krzyzewski

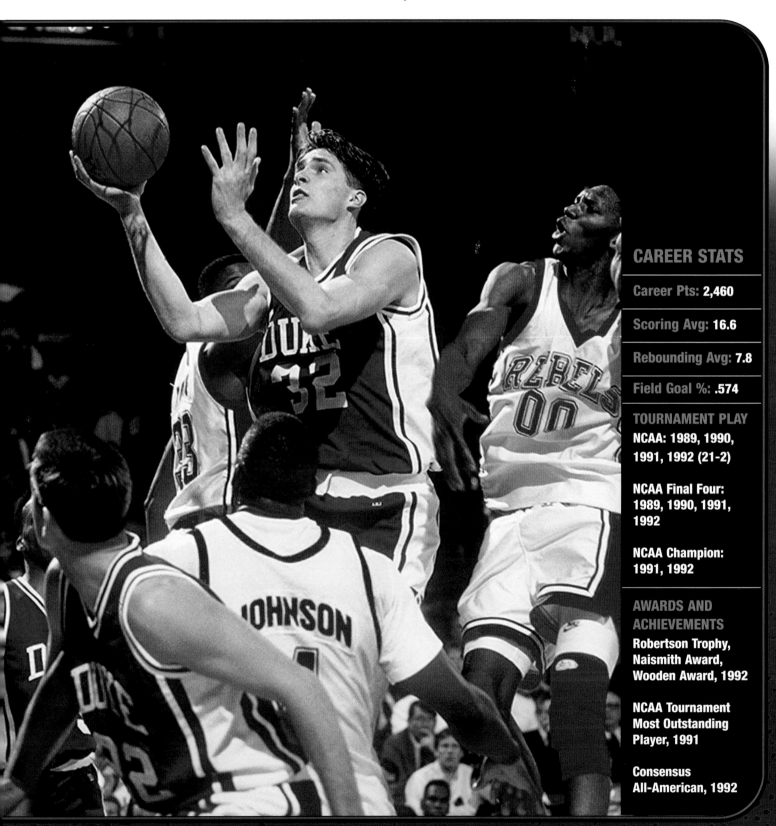

**CAREER STATS**

Career Pts: 2,460

Scoring Avg: 16.6

Rebounding Avg: 7.8

Field Goal %: .574

**TOURNAMENT PLAY**

NCAA: 1989, 1990, 1991, 1992 (21-2)

NCAA Final Four: 1989, 1990, 1991, 1992

NCAA Champion: 1991, 1992

**AWARDS AND ACHIEVEMENTS**

Robertson Trophy, Naismith Award, Wooden Award, 1992

NCAA Tournament Most Outstanding Player, 1991

Consensus All-American, 1992

Height/Weight: 6-11/245   High School: Nichols School, Buffalo   College: Duke University, 1988-1992

# 10 Jerry LUCAS

## CAREER STATS

**Career Pts: 1,990**

**Scoring Avg: 24.3**

**Rebounding Avg: 17.2**

**Field Goal %: .624**

### TOURNAMENT PLAY
**NCAA: 1960, 1961, 1962 (10-2)**

**NCAA Final Four: 1960, 1961, 1962**

**NCAA Champion: 1960**

### AWARDS AND ACHIEVEMENTS
**U.S. Basketball Writers Player of the Year, 1962**

**U.S. Basketball Writers Player of the Year, 1961**

**NCAA Tournament Most Outstanding Player, 1961**

**NCAA Tournament Most Outstanding Player, 1960**

**Consensus All-American, 1962**

**Consensus All-American, 1961**

**Consensus All-American, 1960**

*Born: March 30, 1940, Middletown, Ohio*

## "The most unselfish player that ever played."

—Pete Newell

Long before he gained national fame as the center on Ohio State's greatest teams, Jerry Lucas was a star. He was the top player in Ohio prep basketball as a sophomore starter for Middletown High's state champions, led a second championship as a junior and, as a senior, was named Parade All-American. His recruitment was among the most hotly contested in a century of college basketball.

It seemed the only way to keep him off the stage was by regulation. As a freshman, NCAA rules excluded him from competing with the varsity. When he got the chance to join the Buckeyes as a sophomore, he was an instant All-American: 26.3 points, 16.4 rebounds, a 25-3 record and the program's first NCAA championship. Bob Knight, who played for those Buckeyes and later coached Indiana, called Lucas "the best player that I've ever seen in the Big Ten." That covered nearly four decades.

Given that he became a Rhodes Scholar and a U.S. senator, it is easy to make the case that Princeton's Bill Bradley was the smartest man to play great basketball. Lucas might have been the smartest great player. He studied his opponents and identified their tendencies. He developed his acumen as a rebounder with a bizarre practice routine. He would stand in an empty gym and purposefully miss shots so he could catalogue the angles at which the ball bounced off the rim. Lucas ranks as one of the top 25 rebounders in Division I history and three times grabbed at least 30 in a game. He did it not to gain more attention by taking advantage of inferior opponents. He did it against Indiana, Kentucky and UCLA.

With Lucas at center, Ohio State compiled a 78-6 record and reached the NCAA championship game three consecutive years. He was an eager passer whom legendary coach Pete Newell called "the most unselfish player that ever played." Though he remained a productive scorer throughout his career, he almost was proud that his scoring average declined.

"The team always has been paramount," Lucas told the Columbus Dispatch when his No. 11 OSU jersey was retired. "I could have taken many, many more shots. It wasn't important to me."

*Height/Weight: 6-8/225    High School: Middletown High    College: Ohio State University, 1959-1962*

# 11 Magic JOHNSON

## CAREER STATS

**Career Pts: 1,059**

**Scoring Avg: 17.1**

**Rebounding Avg: 7.6**

**Assists: 7.9**

### TOURNAMENT PLAY
**NCAA: 1979 (5-0)**

**NCAA Final Four: 1979**

**NCAA Champion: 1979**

### AWARDS AND ACHIEVEMENTS
**NCAA Tournament Most Outstanding Player, 1979**

**Consensus All-American, 1979**

*Born: Aug. 14, 1959, Lansing, Mich.*

## When he was a Spartan, he was neither a shooter nor a scorer. He was a player.

There has only been one unique basketball player: Michigan State's Earvin "Magic" Johnson. No one else could have been an All-American at five positions. No one stood with a power forward's body and controlled a game like the best of point guards.

Johnson played with a selfless joy infectious to spectators, teammates and sometimes opponents. His wide smile and constant chatter welcomed anyone who wished to join the celebration of Michigan State's 1979 championship season, a title he conjured with his passing and command of the game.

In two seasons with the Spartans, he helped change how basketball was appreciated. There were many great passers before: Bob Cousy, Oscar Robertson and even Pete Maravich. There was one playing at the same time, Larry Bird, whose Indiana State team became Michigan State's victim in the '79 title game. What they had in common that Johnson did not share was exceptional shooting ability.

At Michigan State, Johnson controlled games in which he struggled to make a shot. He most often flicked the ball at the goal from a low angle, causing it to graze the rim. His size permitted him to collect baskets in the lane and his direction of the fastbreak often resulted in layups. But when he was a Spartan, he was neither a shooter nor a scorer. He was a player.

Before there was a common term for such a thing, Johnson recorded double-figure totals in points, rebounds and assists—a triple-double—in two of the five games that earned Michigan State its first national championship. As the Spartans advanced, clearly a result of Johnson's superb play, spectators had no choice but to redefine their view of basketball greatness. The guy who scored an abundance of points was important, but someone managing every development on the court was of greater value.

Following the title-game victory over Indiana State, Johnson left the Spartans to enter the NBA draft. His success led to a surge of 6-7 and 6-8 players who fancied themselves as point guards. Every tall young man who could dribble and pass would be compared to Johnson. There is only one such player. There is no one like Magic.

**Height/Weight:** 6-9/220   **High School:** Everett High, Lansing   **College:** Michigan State University, 1977-1979

# 12

# Danny MANNING

## CAREER STATS

**Career Pts: 2,951**    **Scoring Avg: 20.1**    **Rebounding Avg: 8.1**    **Field Goal %: .593**    **TOURNAMENT PLAY** NCAA: 1985, 1986, 198
1988 (13-3); NCAA Final Four: 1986, 1988; NCAA Championship: 1988    **AWARDS AND ACHIEVEMENTS** Naismith Award, Wooden Awar
1988; Consensus All-American, 1988; Consensus All-American, 1987; NCAA Tournament Most Outstanding Player, 1988

*Born: May 17, 1966, Hattiesburg, Miss.*

> ## *"He was doing the thing we needed him to do—that was taking charge."*
> —Chris Piper

The Kansas team that achieved an unexpected NCAA championship in 1988 was not a one-man show. "Everybody else on our team knew they did something that enabled us to win," said Chris Piper, the power forward for those Jayhawks. But it was a measure of Danny Manning's excellence that so many perceived that group as "Danny and the Miracles."

With a small forward's ball skills and the size of a center, Manning was successful all four years at Kansas: three-time Big Eight player of the year, two-time All-American and once national player of the year. He scored in double figures in 132 of his 147 games and established a conference points record. There never was a question he would play great; getting him to star was the challenge for coach Larry Brown.

He was not a dominant player during the course of the 1987-88 season, when the Jayhawks went through a losing streak that left them with a 12-8 record. When a strong finish rescued an NCAA bid, they arrived with minimal expectations.

"No way we were thinking we could win it," Piper said. "When you play alongside a guy as great as Danny, you take it for granted. You don't look at the lineup and say, 'We've got Danny Manning; that's going to make the difference.' "

When the Jayhawks reached the tournament's round of 16, Manning began to sense an opportunity. He played feverishly against Vanderbilt, scoring 38 points on 16-of-29 shooting. Just before halftime of that game, he took a badly conceived shot that missed—and drew a pat on the back from Brown.

"He was doing the thing we needed him to do," Piper said. "That was taking charge."

In the Final Four, Manning averaged 28 points. He carried the Jayhawks from a 50-all halftime tie to an 83-79 victory against top-ranked Oklahoma in the title game with 31 points and 18 rebounds. He stepped out of character—and onto the stage where the winner's trophy is presented.

There have been 50 players in NCAA history who topped 2,500 career points. Manning is the only one with a championship ring. He couldn't have done it alone, but he came darned close.

**Height/Weight:** 6-10/230   **High School:** Lawrence (Kansas) High   **College:** University of Kansas, 1984-1988

# 13 Jerry WEST

The great Pete Newell was not a coach who would be lured into the same predicament twice. As California's coach in the 1959 NCAA championship game, he watched junior All-American Jerry West carry West Virginia from a double-digit deficit and nearly cost the Golden Bears a national title. This sort of thing would not happen again.

When Cal faced West Virginia the following season, Newell instructed defenders to completely deny West access to the basketball. It worked. West scored eight points and the Mountaineers otherwise presented no challenge, but Newell learned something about the qualities that made West great.

"In a losing cause, Jerry never started playing for himself. He kept on playing team ball," Newell told *Look* magazine. "For a boy to do that on a rough night was wonderful."

West did not surrender in that defeat because his team often recovered from despair. In the Mountaineers' Final Four season, 14 of their 29 victories required second-half comebacks. "Mr. Clutch" was not a nickname of convenience, conceived after one or two last-second buzzer-beaters. It defined his career.

In his first year with the Mountaineers varsity, he concocted last-second heroics that led them to a 26-2 record and the NCAA Tournament. Against Richmond, he scored with 12 seconds left to force overtime, then produced seven of the team's nine points to secure the victory. He scored 17 of WVU's final 23 points in a comeback from a 14-point deficit against Villanova. He contributed 21 second-half points at Penn State to help his team climb from a 10-point halftime deficit.

West had long arms that aided him as a defender and rebounder. He was a remarkable athlete—described as a "jumping jack" in the *New York Times*—and was as important to West Virginia for his ballhandling and boardwork as his point production. Joe Lapchick, then coach at St. John's, called West "everything a coach could want."

West Virginia was a Southern Conference power when West enrolled, but he delivered three of the program's greatest seasons: a combined 81-12, including the program's only Final Four appearance. West scored 28 points in the biggest game of his Mountaineers career. He made a believer of Newell.

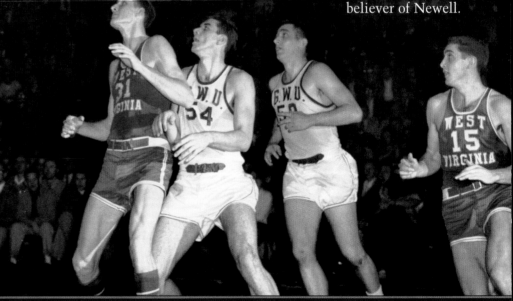

*Born: May 28, 1938, Chelyan, W.Va.*

*"In a losing cause, Jerry never started playing for himself. He kept on playing team ball."*

— Pete Newell

**CAREER STATS**

Career Pts: **2,309**

Scoring Avg: **24.8**

Rebounding Avg: **13.3**

Field Goal %: **.508**

**TOURNAMENT PLAY**
**NCAA: 1958, 1959, 1960 (5-3)**

**NCAA Final Four: 1959**

**AWARDS AND ACHIEVEMENTS**

**NCAA Tournament Most Outstanding Player, 1959**

**Consensus All-American, 1960**

**Consensus All-American, 1959**

*Height/Weight: 6-3/180    High School: East Bank (W.Va.) High    College: West Virginia University, 1957-1960*

# 14 Wilt CHAMBERLAIN

It may not be possible to be too rich or too thin, but Wilt Chamberlain would have argued a basketball player could be too tall or too good. He towered over his competition to such an extent gargantuan achievements were expected to be routine.

They nearly were. Chamberlain was such a gifted athlete that he joined the Jayhawks' track team and won the Big Eight high jump championship with almost no practice time. He scored 52 points and got 31 rebounds against Northwestern in the first game he played with the Kansas varsity. Leaping above the defense, extending his arm and dropping the ball into the goal with his trademark finger roll move, Chamberlain rang up enough points to rank fourth in the nation in scoring as a sophomore. He carried the Jayhawks to the 1957 NCAA championship game—a game they would lose—and was named most outstanding player.

North Carolina, which entered with a perfect record, needed three overtimes to prevail. While the Tar Heels surrounded Chamberlain with four defenders, he scored 23 points and collected 14 rebounds. He shot 6-of-13 from the field, but the other Jayhawks were a collective 9-of-34. Somehow, the loss came to be viewed as Chamberlain's responsibility. He was disappointed enough to consider leaving school.

There always seemed to be something about his Kansas experience that wasn't quite right. Chamberlain sometimes felt out of place as an African American in the Midwest, far removed from his Philadelphia home. Coach Phog Allen had recruited Chamberlain but was forced into mandatory retirement before Wilt made his varsity debut. Chamberlain was not as comfortable with replacement Dick Harp.

As a junior, Chamberlain led Kansas to an 18-5 record and No. 7 poll ranking, but Kansas State earned the Big Eight title and NCAA Tournament bid. That disappointment and the raging frustration of being targeted by college defenses persuaded Chamberlain to leave and earn money with the Harlem Globetrotters.

Chamberlain did not return to the KU campus for nearly 40 years, until he was invited back in 1998 to see his No. 13 jersey retired. Fearing a cool reception, he was greeted with a thunderous standing ovation. His college career at last had an appropriate end.

*He towered over his competition to such an extent gargantuan achievements were expected to be routine.*

**Born:** Aug. 21, 1936, Philadelphia  **Died:** Oct. 12, 1999
**Height/Weight:** 7-1/225  **High School:** Overbrook High,
Philadelphia  **College:** University of Kansas, 1956-1958

## CAREER STATS

**Career Pts:** 1,433

**Scoring Avg:** 29.9

**Rebounding Avg:** 18.3

**Field Goal %:** .470

**TOURNAMENT PLAY**
NCAA: 1957 (3-1)  NCAA
Final Four: 1957

**AWARDS AND ACHIEVEMENTS**

NCAA Tournament
Most Outstanding
Player, 1957

Consensus All-
American, 1958

Consensus All-
American, 1957

# 15

# Patrick EWING

The most promising heavyweight matchup of the 1980s did not involve Larry Holmes, Mike Tyson or Michael Spinks. It was staged between Georgetown's Patrick Ewing and Houston's Akeem Olajuwon and was, according to one of the combatants, no contest.

"It wasn't me and Akeem," Ewing said. "Basketball is a team game, so it wasn't me outplaying him. It was the whole team: Michael Jackson, Michael Graham. My team outplayed his team. That was the reason we won."

Olajuwon entered the 1984 NCAA championship game as the nation's leader in rebounding and field-goal percentage. Long before anyone in the U.S. had learned to spell Olajuwon's name, Ewing had been hailed as the game's next great center. With everything in place for a classic showdown, instead a basketball game developed. Ewing scored 10 points and grabbed nine rebounds. Olajuwon scored 15 and matched Ewing on the boards. But Georgetown won comfortably, claiming Ewing's one national title.

"Winning the championship: that's what it's all about," Ewing said. "It's what everybody strives for when they first start out in the game. I got there three times and was able to come away with one. So that one means a lot, a whole lot."

Ewing was the object of perhaps the fiercest recruiting battle the game has seen. Lew Alcindor was held in greater esteem, but more programs were taking the game seriously by the time Ewing arrived with his long arms, natural strength and aptitude for defense.

Coach John Thompson prevailed in that scrum; this helped establish Georgetown as a national basketball power. Ewing did not become a versatile and prolific scorer until he entered the NBA. At Georgetown, he never averaged 18 points, but then, he attempted fewer than 10 shots per game. What Ewing was, was a presence. When he was on the floor, opponents could not help but be consumed with his presence.

Though Georgetown remained a top program for years after Ewing completed his career, it never reached the Final Four without him. "There were a lot of things coach Thompson taught me about life," he said. "If I had to do it all over again, that would still be my choice."

*Born: August 5, 1962, Kingston, Jamaica*

> *"It wasn't me and Akeem. Basketball is a team game ... It was the whole team: Michael Jackson, Michael Graham. My team outplayed his team. That was the reason we won."*
>
> — Patrick Ewing

## CAREER STATS

**Career Pts: 2,184**   **Scoring Avg: 15.3**   **Rebounding Avg: 9.2**   **Field Goal %: .620**   **TOURNAMENT PLAY**   NCAA: 1982, 1983, 1984, 1985 (15-3); NCAA Final Four: 1982, 1984, 1985; NCAA Champion: 1984   **AWARDS AND ACHIEVEMENTS** Naismith Award, 1985; Consensus All-American, 1985; Consensus All-American, 1984; Consensus All-American, 1983

ght/Weight: 7-0/245   High School: Rindge & Latin High, Cambridge, Mass.   College: Georgetown University, 1981-1985

# 16 michael JORDAN

It is easy to forget how good he was. The memory fades. The numbers lie. To some wishing to rewrite history, Michael Jordan becomes an ordinary college player. Those who were there believed otherwise.

When THE SPORTING NEWS named Jordan player of the year as a North Carolina sophomore, Georgia Tech center Tim Harvey said competing against him was "like watching Superman. There's nothing you can do but stand and look at him." Years later, Duke center Jay Bilas recalled how teammate Bill Jackman talked incessantly of Jordan's dominance following 32 points against the Blue Devils in 1983. "In the locker room, on the bus," said Bilas. "David Henderson finally had to tell him to shut up, because we had to play them five more times. You had to compete against him."

Jordan's achievements after leaving college became so enormous they dwarfed all other players—and his own college record. Because he was an NBA scoring champion but not a career 20-point player at North Carolina, because the Tar Heels did not return to the Final Four his last two seasons, his impact at Carolina was questioned.

Coach Dean Smith's revered system might have constrained Jordan's productivity, but it elevated his understanding and fundamental skills. And he was amazing as a Tar Heel. "We all knew at the time that Jordan was the best player," Bilas said. Jordan recovered from a broken wrist early in his sophomore year to average 20 points and produce several game-breaking plays, including a steal and 22-foot shot to force overtime against Tulane.

He was unchallenged as the best NCAA player during his junior year. Jordan flew high above the humans attempting to defend him, but what separated Jordan was his body control and uncommon competitive steak. That quality led Smith to call Jordan aside following a timeout huddle in the closing seconds of the 1982 NCAA championship game and instructed him to confidently fire the shot that would give Carolina the lead over Georgetown.

From the left corner, he rolled a 17-footer off his fingertips and into the goal. It was the championship winner. This marked the unofficial launch of basketball's greatest career.

*Born: Feb. 17, 1963, Brooklyn, N.Y.*

# Jordan's achievements after leaving college became so enormous they dwarfed all other players—and his own college record.

## Why #16?

Michael Jordan is the sport's best player, but he built toward that superiority gradually. He was a terrific player as a sophomore and better as a junior, but fits here because his opportunities to elevate his team were limited.

## CAREER STATS

**Career Pts:** 1,788    **Scoring Avg:** 17.7    **Rebounding Avg:** 5.0    **Field Goal %:** .540

**TOURNAMENT PLAY** NCAA: 1982, 1983, 1984 (8-2); NCAA Final Four: 1982; NCAA Champion: 1982

**AWARDS AND ACHIEVEMENTS** Robertson Trophy, Naismith Award, Wooden Award, 1984; The Sporting News Player of the Year, 1983; Consensus All-American, 1984; Consensus All-American, 1983

*Height/Weight:* 6-6/200    *High School:* Emsley A. Laney High, Wilmington, N.C.    *College:* University of North Carolina, 1981-1984

# 17 Tom GOLA

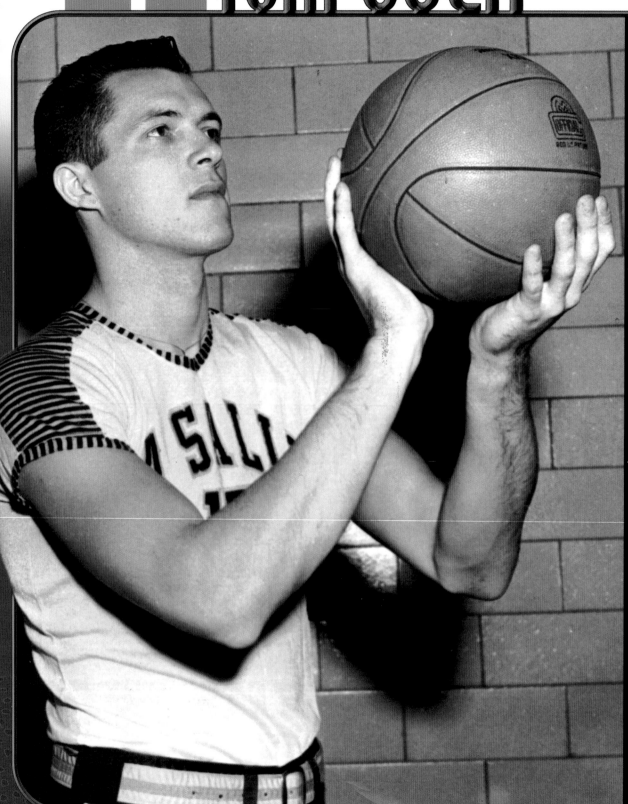

## CAREER STATS

**Career Pts: 2,462**

**Scoring Avg: 20.9**

**Rebounding Avg: 18.7**

**Field Goal %: .407**

### TOURNAMENT PLAY
**NCAA: 1954, 1955 (9-1)**

**NCAA Final Four: 1954, 1955**

**NCAA Champion: 1954**

**NIT: 1952, 1953**

**NIT Champion: 1952**

### AWARDS AND ACHIEVEMENTS
**United Press International Player of the Year, 1955**

**NCAA Tournament Most Outstanding Player, 1954**

**NIT Most Valuable Player, 1952**

**Consensus All-American, 1955**

**Consensus All-American, 1954**

**Consensus All-American, 1953**

*Born: Jan. 13, 1933, Philadelphia*

> ## "He was Magic Johnson before Magic Johnson—a big guy who could handle the ball and do it all."
> — Sonny Hill

Had LaSalle not been so small when Tom Gola arrived, it would have taken him a little longer to turn the college into a basketball giant.

When Gola enrolled in 1951, freshmen were ineligible for varsity competition. He received a waiver because La Salle's enrollment numbered fewer than 1,000. When he led the Explorers in scoring and rebounding and they earned an NIT championship, it was apparent how big an advantage that was.

LaSalle reached postseason tournaments in each of Gola's seasons and played for a national title in all but his sophomore year, 1953, when he was injured in an NIT loss to St. John's and played barely half the game. He still scored 17 points.

In the 1954 NCAA championship game, Gola contributed 19 points as the Explorers stormed from a one-point halftime deficit to leave Bradley far behind. A select group of American players has won championships at the high school, college and professional levels. Gola did it in the same town: a city title at La Salle High, an NCAA title at LaSalle College, an NBA title with the Philadelphia Warriors.

LaSalle lost only 19 games during Gola's career, the last of those when Bill Russell's powerful San Francisco squad prevented the Explorers from claiming consecutive NCAA championships.

Gola had slim shoulders but long, strong arms and exceptionally fast hands. He used his quickness and strength to gain position under the boards. He ranked third in the nation in rebounding as a junior and eighth as a senior and remains the NCAA's career leader in rebounds. His coach with the Explorers, Ken Loeffler, called Gola "Mr. All-Around"—not so catchy, but accurate enough.

When the NIT named its all-time team upon celebrating its 50th anniversary, Gola was ranked among the five best players to compete in the tournament. Philadelphia native Wilt Chamberlain claimed Gola was the greatest player the city produced.

Basketball commentator Sonny Hill, who has observed the Philadelphia scene for a half-century, once said he'd never seen a college player with the variety of skills Gola mastered. "He was Magic Johnson before Magic Johnson—a big guy who could handle the ball and do it all," Hill said. "He was multi-dimensional."

**Height/Weight:** 6-6/200   **High School:** La Salle High   **College:** La Salle College, 1951-1955

# 18 Isiah THOMAS

## CAREER STATS

**Career Pts: 968**

**Scoring Avg: 15.4**

**Assists: 5.7**

**Field Goal %: .534**

### TOURNAMENT PLAY
**NCAA: 1980, 1981 (6-1)**

**NCAA Final Four: 1981**

**NCAA Champion: 1981**

### AWARDS AND ACHIEVEMENTS
**NCAA Tournament Most Outstanding Player, 1981**

**Consensus All-American, 1981**

*Born: April 30, 1961, Chicago*

*Thomas was spectacular because of the absence of flash. He would neglect the opportunity to make a dazzling pass if a sensible option was available.*

For 29 years, the Indiana program belonged to Bob Knight. The Hoosiers employed his offense, his defense, his method of operation. They were his team. The two seasons he had Isiah Thomas in the lineup might have been the only point in his career when he was willing to share a bit of his authority.

Thomas adapted to the Knight system. He ran the grandly efficient motion offense and learned to play Indiana's brand of man-to-man defense. Yet Thomas' command of the game and the team were so absolute he was granted unprecedented power in leading the Hoosiers' attack.

That may be the most notable achievement in Thomas' Indiana career. His greatness is not obvious in statistical totals. In two years, he did not reach 1,000 career points. Knight's offense, which did not demand the point guard create frequent scoring opportunities, limited Thomas' assists. His teams won 73 percent of their games, not an overwhelming rate of success.

Those Hoosiers did win titles, and that was attributable to Thomas' leadership. Knight named him captain in December of his sophomore season, and Indiana progressed from 7-5 against non-conference competition to Big Ten champion. In the 1981 Final Four, Thomas outclassed LSU star Ethan Martin and North Carolina's reliable Jimmy Black by shooting 56 percent from the field and averaging 18.5 points. Indiana won the five games that resulted in the national championship by an average of 21.8 points. North Carolina coach Dean Smith called Thomas one of the greatest point guards in college basketball history.

Thomas was spectacular because of the absence of flash. He would neglect the opportunity to make a dazzling pass if a sensible option was available. His quickness did not assault the senses; he maneuvered so smoothly it was difficult to fathom how he moved so fast from one place to the next.

The conversion of Thomas from gifted point guard prospect to great Indiana point guard did not happen immediately. Thomas had to endure a few of Knight's infamous harangues before he recognized what was being demanded of him. When that arrived, Knight had at his disposal the greatest player he would ever enjoy coaching. And Indiana owned another NCAA title.

**Height/Weight: 6-1/175    High School: St. Joseph's, Westchester, Ill.    College: Indiana University, 1979-1981**

# 19 Elgin BAYLOR

## CAREER STATS

**Career Pts: 1,686**

**Scoring Avg: 31.2**

**Rebounding Avg: 19.8**

**Field Goal %: .498**

## TOURNAMENT PLAY
**NCAA: 1958 (4-1)**

**NCAA Final Four: 1958**

**NIT: 1957**

## AWARDS AND ACHIEVEMENTS
**NCAA Tournament Most Outstanding Player, 1958**

**Consensus All-American, 1958**

*Born: Sept. 16, 1934, Washington, D.C.    Height/Weight:  6-5/225    High School: Spingarn High, Washington*

# He was 'The Man With 1,000 Moves,' one of the most dazzling scorers of his or any decade.

Of the 88 programs that have navigated through the NCAA Tournament to land in the Final Four, only three no longer compete at the Division I level. City College of New York never fully recovered from the point-shaving scandals of the 1950s, and New York University de-emphasized basketball. Seattle simply ran out of Elgin Baylors.

He was "The Man With 1,000 Moves," one of the most dazzling scorers of his or any decade. He is recognized for helping to take the game from the floor to the air, an important link in the evolutionary chain that eventually led to Connie Hawkins, Julius Erving and Michael Jordan. For Baylor, it was more a matter of his ability to manufacture shots while floating above the court than ramming them through the goal. He rarely dunked. Baylor was at his best when faking a defender and driving past him. It wasn't the end of the play that electrified fans, but the start.

Baylor nearly began his athletic career in football at the College of Idaho, so it was no surprise he controlled basketball games with his strength. He was expert at backing down defenders, using his dribble to draw ever closer to the goal. He rebounded at a furious pace and led the nation in 1956-57, his first varsity season after transferring to Seattle, despite standing several inches shorter than stars Wilt Chamberlain of Kansas and Charlie Tyra of Louisville.

He ranked third in scoring and Seattle finished fifth in the final polls, but Baylor was not familiar enough to crack the All-American team. Basketball followers got a clear picture the following season, when Seattle reached the 1958 NCAA championship game before losing to Kentucky.

Baylor's 91 tournament rebounds are the third-best total in the event's history. His 35-foot shot at the buzzer gave him 35 points and beat San Francisco in the 1958 West Region semifinals. In the semifinals at the Final Four, against the imposing Kansas State frontcourt led by forward Bob Boozer, Baylor wrecked a three-defender rotation to finish with 23 points in a blowout victory. Kansas State coach Tex Winter had a simple message afterward: "He beat us." Baylor could make a program and break one, too.

*College: College of Idaho - Seattle University, 1956-1958*

# 20 George MIKAN

There had been tall men in basketball before George Mikan played at DePaul, but he became the first true giant of the game. He stood within a couple inches of the magic 7-foot mark, reaching far closer to the rim than any great player who preceded him. His eventual dominance made the search for the gifted big man an eternal quest for teams seeking to excel.

The development process was difficult for Mikan. He arrived at DePaul almost uninvited, wearing glasses that served to accentuate the perception he was slow and awkward. "We just wanted him to go into a corner and just get lost," his coach, Ray Meyer, later told the *Chicago Sun-Times*. It was not easy for a player of Mikan's size to hide, though, and Meyer came to understand the value of a center who could tower over opponents without tripping over his feet.

Meyer had Mikan train hard to improve his conditioning, much like a boxer. The coach devised what came to be known as the Mikan drill, in which a player darts back-and-forth across the lane, banking short hook shots off the backboard with either hand. This enhanced Mikan's stamina, footwork and touch. In his first varsity season, Mikan averaged a healthy 11.3 points. He scored 20 points in his first NCAA Tournament game, a victory over Dartmouth. It also was the first time he reached that mark. This soon became routine.

During the next three seasons, he scored 20 or more points 42 times in 74 games. In the 1945 NIT, Mikan averaged 40 points, including a 53-point performance in a semifinal victory over Rhode Island. He led the nation in scoring as a junior (23.3) and senior (23.1). None of the other great players of the World War II era—Charles Black of Kansas, Arnie Ferrin of Utah, Bob Kurland of Oklahoma A&M—averaged 20 points in his best season.

Only slightly behind in his development as a center, Kurland was even taller than Mikan. The two players faced each other five times, with DePaul winning three of the games and Mikan outscoring his counterpart, 15.4 points per game to 12.8. Together, they helped make college basketball a bigger sport.

**Born:** June 18, 1924, Joliet, Ill.  **Height/Weight:** 6-10/245  **High School:** Quigley Prep, Chicago  **College:** DePaul University, 1942-1946

*"We just wanted him to go into a corner and just get lost."*

— Ray Meyer

## CAREER STATS

**Career Pts:** 1,870

**Scoring Avg:** 19.1

**Free Throw %:** .680

### TOURNAMENT PLAY
**NCAA:** 1943 (1-1)

**NCAA Final Four:** 1943

**NIT:** 1944, 1945

**NIT Champion:** 1945

### AWARDS AND ACHIEVEMENTS
**Helms Foundation Player of the Year, 1944**

**NIT Most Valuable Player, 1945**

**Consensus All-American, 1946**

**Consensus All-American, 1945**

**Consensus All-American, 1944**

# 21 BiLL BRADLEY

The game for which Bill Bradley may be best remembered didn't really amount to much. Princeton and Wichita State did not want to lose the NCAA third-place game, but neither did it matter which side won. They were required to play, so Bradley put on a show with 58 points and 17 rebounds that helped him to claim the Most Outstanding Player at the 1965 Final Four.

"I noticed that players were throwing me the ball. And I threw it right back to them," Bradley told THE SPORTING NEWS. "And then the coach called a timeout and he said, 'Look, this is your last game. Go ahead and shoot.' And I did."

Bradley set the single-game Final Four scoring record, but there were better demonstrations of his brilliance. In a first-round escape of Penn State, Bradley scored 13 of his 22 points in the last eight minutes to rescue Princeton from a 45-42 deficit. In the East Region final, he hit 14-of-20 shots from the field and all 13 of his free throws for 41 points in an overwhelming dismissal of Providence, No. 4 in the polls. That was a great player at his best.

The sight of Princeton in the Final Four was no less astounding in 1965, save for the fact Bradley was in its lineup. As a prep star in Missouri, his genius as a player had been no secret to recruiters. He received dozens of scholarship offers, including one from Kentucky, but rejected all to attend Princeton. The Tigers won the Ivy League championship three consecutive years and played at the game's highest levels.

Bradley never scored fewer than 16 points in a game. He scored because Princeton could not win without it. He mastered the jump shots required of a perimeter player and the post moves and hooks upon which the smaller centers of his era relied. He was a sophisticated passer, averaging 7.0 assists in the first two rounds of the 1965 tournament, and was dedicated to team principles. It is curious the game that brought him the greatest fame saw him play, just once, for himself. There was so much more to Bill Bradley.

*Born: July 28, 1943, Crystal City, Mo.*

*He mastered the jump shots required of a perimeter player and the post moves and hooks upon which the smaller centers of his era relied. He was a sophisticated passer ... and was dedicated to team principles.*

## CAREER STATS

**Career Pts:** 2,503

**Scoring Avg:** 30.2

**Rebounding Avg:** 12.1

**Field Goal %:** .513

### TOURNAMENT PLAY
**NCAA: 1963, 1964, 1965 (5-4)**

**NCAA Final Four: 1965**

### AWARDS AND ACHIEVEMENTS
**Oscar Robertson Trophy, 1965**

**NCAA Tournament Most Outstanding Player, 1965**

**Consensus All-American, 1965**

**Consensus All-American, 1964**

*Height/Weight: 6-5/205    High School: Crystal City High    College: Princeton University, 1962-1965*

# 22 Phil FORD

There never has been a more ideal marriage between strategy and star than that between North Carolina point guard Phil Ford and coach Dean Smith's Four Corners offense. When Smith signaled the strategy by holding his hand into the air with four fingers aloft, Ford became both conductor (coordinating his teammates' movements like a symphony) and surgeon (cutting into opponents and removing their hope). It was such a perfect fit some nicknamed this tactic the "Ford Corners."

The Four Corners positioned Ford near the midcourt line, with one teammate at each corner of the offensive zone. The indicated use for this approach was as a delay game to protect late leads. With Ford, the Tar Heels could control the course of a game.

Ford's speed prevented opponents from catching him as he dribbled, and his strength deterred them from knocking him off the ball if they came close. Ford could dominate the ball for several minutes at a time, searching for an instant when a defender would lose interest or slip off-balance. Then, he would drive for a layup or dump a pass to one of several gifted teammates.

"It would frustrate the other team," Ford said.

The Tar Heels won three ACC regular-season titles and three tournament titles in his four seasons. Ford's success as a scorer is a testament to his mastery of the Four Corners. It cut down on his team's output, but he is the school's career points leader.

Though it was the stuff of genius, both Smith's and Ford's, the Four Corners was not popular—especially among opposing fans. When it backfired in the 1977 NCAA title-game loss to Marquette, many journalists covering the game gleefully derided the coach and his invention.

Ford later did some announcing on North Carolina radio broadcasts and called a 2002 ACC Tournament game in which the Heels stalled by using a version of the Four Corners. As sophomore point guard Adam Boone stood where Ford once dribbled the ball, he was loudly booed. "I know just how he feels," Ford said over the air.

Such is the curse of the visionary artist. Sometimes, the public doesn't appreciate the work until it's too late.

*Born: Feb. 9, 1956, Rocky Mount, N.C.*

**Ford became both conductor (coordinating his teammates' movements like a symphony) and surgeon (cutting into opponents and removing their hope).**

## CAREER STATS

Career Pts: **2,290**

Scoring Avg: **18.6**

Field Goal %: **.527**

Assists: **6.1**

**TOURNAMENT PLAY**
NCAA: 1975, 1976, 1977, 1978 (5-4)

NCAA Final Four: 1977

**AWARDS AND ACHIEVEMENTS**
Robertson Trophy, 1978

Wooden Award, 1978 Consensus

All-American, 1978 Consensus

All-American, 1977

*Height/Weight: 6-2/180    High School: Rocky Mount High   College: University of North Carolina, 1974-1978*

# 23 Rick MOUNT

## CAREER STATS

**Career Pts:** 2,323    **Scoring Avg:** 32.3    **Rebounding:** 2.9    **Field Goal %:** .483    **TOURNAMENT PLAY:  NCAA:** 1969 (3-1)
**NCAA Final Four:** 1969    AWARDS AND ACHIEVEMENTS **Consensus All-American, 1970  Consensus All-American, 1969**

*Born: January 5, 1947, Lebanon, Ind.    Height/Weight: 6-4, 180*

## "If I had a 20-footer and you had a 20-footer, I was going to take the shot."

—Rick Mount

The prettiest jump shot ever seen was constructed in an Indiana garage from materials commonly found around the home. The essential ingredient was an athletic young boy who would grow to stand 6-4 and 180 pounds and become known to the basketball world as Rick Mount.

His father, Pete Mount, was a high school star but did not have the experience to teach his son the basics of the jumper. The technique of his time was the two-handed set shot. But Pete did tell Rick—under penalty of spanking—not to shoot on a regulation basket until he grew a bit. "I never picked up any bad habits," Rick said.

Instead he learned good form by aiming a tennis ball at an empty peanut can. When that goal didn't seem real enough, he fashioned a rim from a coat hanger, cut up one of his father's fishing nets and tacked that contraption to the garage wall.

The lessons Mount learned led him to set the Big Ten scoring record with 61 points in a 1970 game against Iowa. His 32.3 career average also is a league standard. Some of Mount's accomplishments as a scorer were overshadowed by the amazing production of LSU guard Pete Maravich during the same period. However, Maravich shot a dozen more times per game, connected on a lower percentage and never competed in the NCAA Tournament.

Mount's junior-season team featured future pros Billy Keller and Herm Gilliam on the perimeter. Coach George King asked the two seniors to sacrifice individual statistics and provide greater scoring opportunities for Mount. The veterans agreed, and the Boilermakers stormed through the Big Ten season with a 13-1 record. What stopped them from winning an NCAA title was the same force that denied everyone else from 1967 through 1973: the UCLA Bruins.

Mount occasionally was criticized for his defensive work, but coaches had discouraged him from becoming too physical for fear he'd encounter foul trouble. He was a capable passer, but there was one reality that defined Purdue with Mount in its lineup: "If I had a 20-footer and you had a 20-footer," Mount said, "I was going to take the shot."

**High School: Lebanon High     College: Purdue University, 1967-1970**

# 24 Rick BARRY

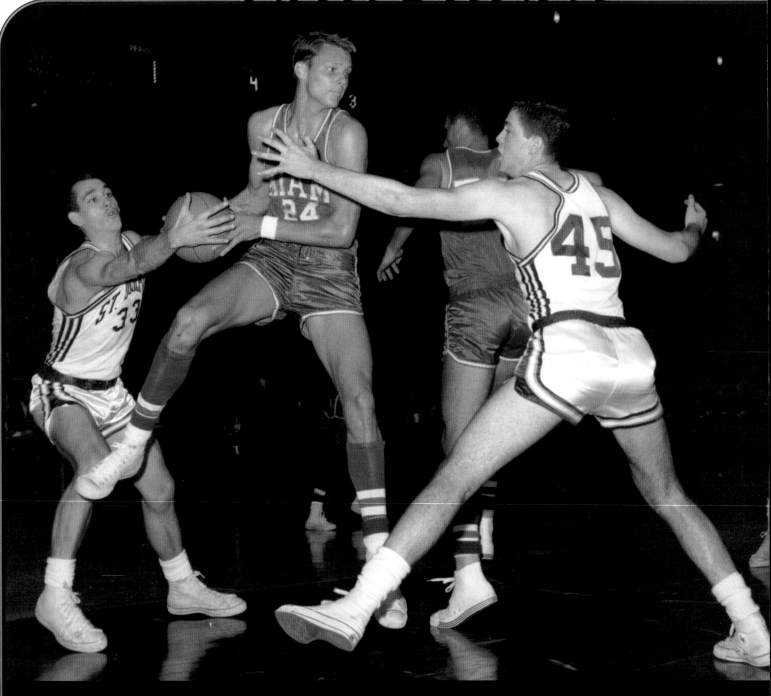

## CAREER STATS

**Career Pts: 2,298**   **Scoring Avg: 29.8**   **Rebounding Avg: 16.5**   **Field Goal %: .522**   **TOURNAMENT PLAY: NIT: 1963, 1964 (1-2)**
**AWARDS AND ACHIEVEMENTS: Consensus All-American, 1965**

*Born: March 28, 1944, Elizabeth, N.J.*

*Though he was a volatile competitor, he was devoted to team success and playing the game properly.*

Miami did not own much tradition before Rick Barry arrived. For a long time after he left, there was almost none that didn't bear his name. Few great players have the courage to take their skills into unexplored territory. Barry always had a pioneer's confidence.

Growing up south of Newark, Barry was eager to live in a warmer and brighter climate and see the rest of the country. "When you live in New Jersey," he said, "you want to get as far away as possible." He liked that Miami competed as an independent, which presented the opportunity to travel to different parts of the country.

Only 17 when he entered college, Barry was encouraged by a brother to attend a school that was not a "basketball factory," where more experienced prospects would be stacked deep on the bench and he might be forced to wait for an opportunity. It was a prudent thought, but it is difficult to imagine a talent such as Barry being buried beneath ordinary athletes.

As a senior, Barry topped 50 points six times and became the nation's leading scorer with his 37.4 average. He subsequently became the only player to top the NCAA, ABA and NBA in that category. He was a master of the mid-range jump shot, working tirelessly to find gaps in the opposing defense and sneaking in to score. His passing helped the Hurricanes average better than 90 points per game. Though he was a volatile competitor, he was devoted to team success and playing the game properly.

Barry had a "nose for the ball" that helped him to average 18.3 rebounds as a senior. Working the offensive boards and scoring on put-backs accounted for a significant portion of his point production. "I was a little more than just a scorer," Barry said.

In three varsity seasons, Barry's teams made two appearances in the NIT and missed a third because of NCAA probation his senior year. That was as successful a period as Miami basketball would enjoy for nearly three decades. The program was eliminated and not revived until the mid-1980s. When the Hurricanes again began competing on the national level, it was Rick Barry's legacy they were trying to match.

*Height/Weight: 6-7/200   High School: Roselle Park (N.J.) High   College: University of Miami, 1962-1965*

# 25 Cazzie RUSSELL

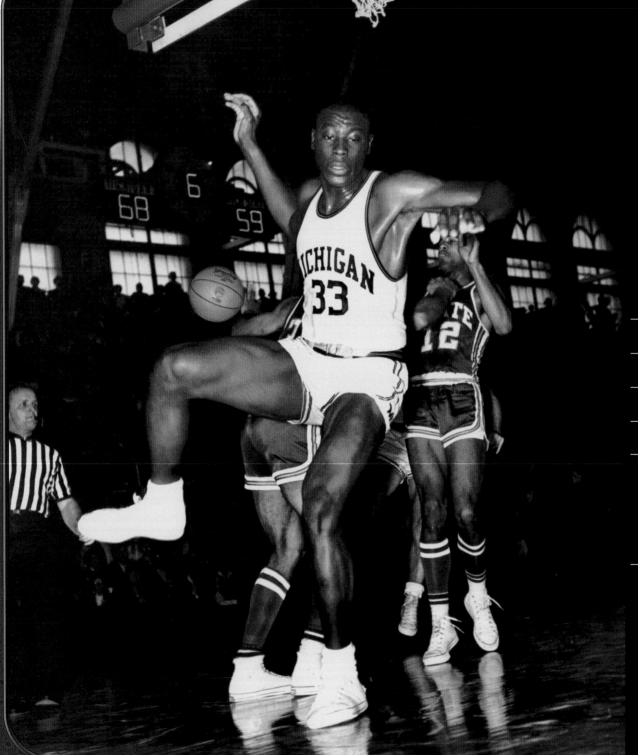

## CAREER STATS

**Career Pts: 2,164**

**Scoring Avg: 27.1**

**Rebounding Avg: 8.5**

**Field Goal %: .505**

## TOURNAMENT PLAY
**NCAA: 1964, 1965, 1966 (6-3)**

**NCAA Final Four: 1964, 1965**

## AWARDS AND ACHIEVEMENTS
**Robertson Trophy, 1966**

**Consensus All-American, 1966**

**Consensus All-American, 1965**

**Born:** *June 7, 1944, Chicago*    **Height/Weight:** *6-5/215*    **High School:** *Carver High, Chicago*    **College:** *University of Michigan, 1963-1966*

## An uncommonly physical guard, Russell was impervious to pressure.

In those moments when he faced a distinct challenge, Cazzie Russell was at his best. If Michigan needed a last-second shot to win, Russell wanted the ball. For the biggest games, he delivered outsized performances. When there was a personal confrontation, the other person had a long night of work ahead.

Russell's two bouts with Princeton's Bill Bradley in 1964-65 were among the most competitive one-on-one battles in the sport's history. They met in the Holiday Festival tournament in New York and again in the Final Four. Neither could decidedly outplay the other, but Michigan left each game with a victory.

The first of those ended with Bradley on the bench after fouling out with 41 points. Russell rallied Michigan with six of the final 12 points, including a 12-foot jumper that provided the Wolverines' two-point margin of victory and left him with 27 points. The second meeting, contested in the Final Four, saw Russell outscored by a single point but Michigan dominating the second half and advancing to the championship game against UCLA.

An uncommonly physical guard, Russell was impervious to pressure. In two national semifinal games and one NCAA title game, he averaged 29 points and shot 59 percent. As a junior, he made a 25-foot jumper just ahead of the buzzer to defeat Wichita State. His jumper tied Indiana with nine seconds left, and he made two free throws to win it in overtime. In the NCAA Tournament, he scored 11 points in the final five minutes to deliver a two-point win over Vanderbilt.

These games were more important than Michigan's game against San Francisco in Chicago during Russell's senior year. But that trip mattered to Russell because it was his first visit to his hometown as a member of the Michigan team. USF coach Pete Peletta publicly suggested Dons star Joe Ellis was prepared to outgun Russell. In the first half, it seemed he was correct. Ellis scored 13 to Russell's 10. Then Russell was reminded the challenge had made headlines that morning. Russell held Ellis to seven points in the final 20 minutes. Russell scored 35.

San Francisco made the mistake of daring Russell to be great.

It was just what he needed.

# 26 Austin CARR

There were two simple reasons none of the other Notre Dame players complained about all those shots Austin Carr fired during the course of a game. First, he made most of them. "I didn't look at it as shooting a lot," he said, "because I always shot over 55 percent from the field." And the Fighting Irish usually won.

Carr's offensive brilliance resulted in three consecutive NCAA Tournament bids for the Irish. That permitted Carr to establish several tournament scoring records, including highest average (41.3) and single-game performance (61 points vs. Ohio University in the 1970 first round). Of the six 50-point games in the tournament's history, Carr produced three.

Carr was a powerful guard who could use his muscle to score around the lane, which was how he earned nearly 10 free throws per game. He did most of his damage, though, by working to free himself for long-range jumpers. He launched 1,925 shots in his career, an average of 26 per game, but that generated scoring averages of 38.1 points in his junior year and 38.0 points as a senior. He fell short of the Division I scoring title each time, finishing behind LSU's Pete Maravich and then Mississippi's Johnny Neumann, but neither of them got to compete in the NCAAs. Carr ranks No. 2 in career scoring average, behind Maravich.

In 74 career games, Carr failed to score in double figures only twice, and one of those resulted when he broke his foot in an NCAA Tournament loss to Miami (Ohio) his sophomore season. In fact, he reached double figures in field goals in 55 of his 58 games as a junior and senior. He maintained that shooting so often was not as easy as it appeared. Given the variety of gimmick defenses designed to stop him—the box-and-one, the triangle-and-two—he needed to be extraordinarily well-conditioned to still be accurate by game's end.

"It was in vogue to be a higher scorer at the time. The coaches didn't mind having one or two players scoring the majority of the points," Carr said. "If a player was open, I would get him the ball. I wouldn't pass up an open player to get a shot."

**Born:** *March 10, 1948, Washington, D.C.*  **Height/Weight:** *6-3/200*  **High School:** *Mackin High, Washington*

> "If a player was open, I would get him the ball. I wouldn't pass up an open player to get a shot."
>
> — Austin Carr

**CAREER STATS**

Career Pts: **2,560**

Scoring Avg: **34.6**

Rebounding Avg: **7.3**

Field Goal %: **.528**

**TOURNAMENT PLAY**
NCAA: 1969, 1970, 1971 (2-3)

**AWARDS AND ACHIEVEMENTS**
Naismith Award, 1971

Consensus All-American, 1971

U.S. Basketball Writers All-American, 1970

*College: Notre Dame University, 1968-1971*

# 27 Bob KURLAND

He did not run the 4-minute mile, did not swat 60 home runs, did not rush for 2,000 yards and, as a basketball player, did not score 100 points in a game. Bob Kurland simply grew, and kept growing, and when he was done reached an odd sort of milestone. He was the game's first great 7-foot center.

Counting the members that entered the club since wouldn't require more than a couple sets of fingers and toes. But Kurland helped demonstrate an abnormally tall person could serve as a basketball weapon if he sufficiently developed his strength and dexterity.

Kurland was a successful high schooler and twice played in the Missouri state championship game, but few colleges were interested in such an unusual player. Hank Iba of Oklahoma A&M, one of the game's brilliant coaches, recognized it would be worth the time to have a true big man on his side.

In his first season, Kurland struggled and played only sporadically, averaging just 2.5 points in 21 games. But he developed rapidly and was a double-figure scorer in each of his last three seasons. His 643 points in 33 games as a senior established a single-season college record.

Kurland's career ran concurrently with that of another oversized center, DePaul's George Mikan, and between them they won three national tournaments. The rule against goaltending, installed in 1945, was introduced with both players in mind. Kurland was less agile than Mikan but also much harder to move. His more balanced team won the NCAA title in 1945 and 1946, with Kurland powering his way to 22 points in the 1945 championship game victory over NYU and 23 of his team's 43 points in beating North Carolina the following season.

Kurland chose not to pursue a professional career, instead beginning a career in the petroleum industry and starring for the AAU Phillips 66ers. Mikan starred with championship teams in the NBA, so he is better remembered, but Kurland was equally important in the evolution of the game. And it was Kurland who left the game with two NCAA championships and the two inches of height that made him an historic figure in the sport.

*Born: Dec. 23, 1924, St. Louis*

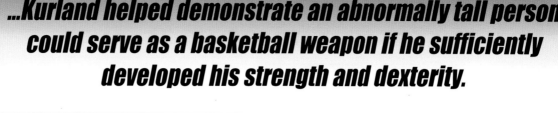

**...Kurland helped demonstrate an abnormally tall person could serve as a basketball weapon if he sufficiently developed his strength and dexterity.**

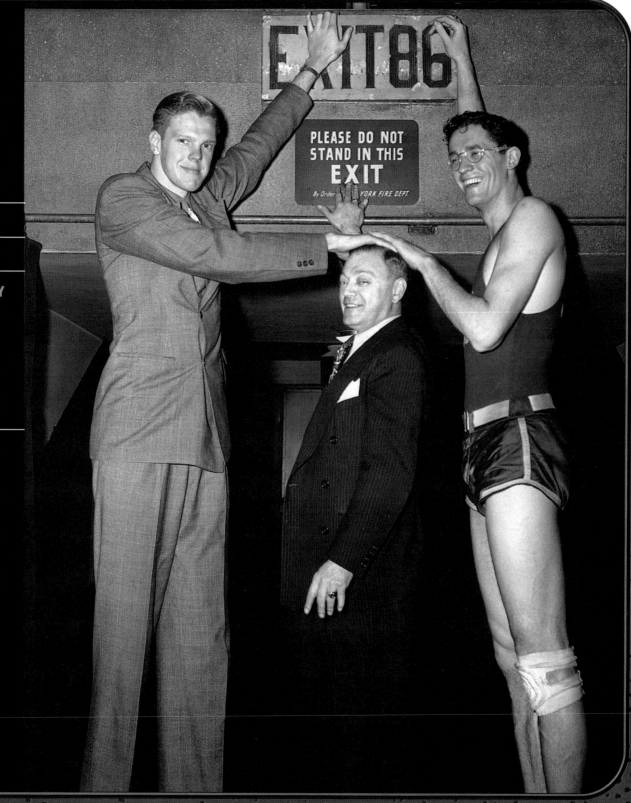

## CAREER STATS

Career Pts: **1,669**

Scoring Avg: **14.1**

**TOURNAMENT PLAY**
NCAA: 1945, 1946
(6-0)

NCAA Final Four:
1945, 1946

NCAA Champion:
1945, 1946

**AWARDS AND ACHIEVEMENTS**
Helms Foundation Player of the Year, 1946

NCAA Tournament Most Outstanding Player, 1946

NCAA Tournament Most Outstanding Player, 1945

Consensus All-American, 1946

Consensus All-American, 1945

Consensus All-American, 1944

*Height/Weight: 7-0/230    High School: Jennings (Mo.) High    College: Oklahoma A&M College, 1942-1946*

# 28 Bobby HURLEY

The shot best remembered from Bobby Hurley's years at Duke was unleashed not by Hurley, but teammate Christian Laettner. The 18-foot, buzzer-beating turnaround jumper that beat Kentucky and sent the Blue Devils to the 1992 Final Four has been replayed on television as often as any sporting moment. Hurley's shot against unbeaten UNLV in 1991 survives mostly in the memories of those who saw it.

Hurley's moment didn't have the same dramatic setting. The clocked showed 2:13 when he dribbled into the defense, ignored the lethal "amoeba" zone the Rebels were setting and nailed a 23-foot 3-pointer from the left wing. That cut deeply into an apparently safe, five-point UNLV lead. The Blue Devils rallied to claim a 79-77 victory in that NCAA semifinal.

"I was just getting ready to call out a play, and Bobby got down the court and just shot it," said Mike Krzyzewski, Hurley's coach at Duke. "Within a flash, this kid hits that shot and gives us life and confidence. And we got our opportunity to beat Kansas and win our first national championship. I think that shot's every bit as big—and it may have been bigger."

It was typical of Hurley to make that decision unilaterally. He was such a commanding point guard Krzyzewski often didn't bother to call plays. Hurley's ballhandling made it superfluous to have an established plan to attack pressure defenses. The call was to get the ball to Hurley.

Hurley was blessed with excellent targets to complete scoring plays, which helped him to become the NCAA's career assists leader. His teams played in three NCAA championship games, and he won more tournament games as a starter than any point guard. Not as quick as some rivals, Hurley prepared to outrun them late in games by training each day on a StairMaster following the Blue Devils' exhausting practice sessions.

"Bobby was the most daring player I ever coached," Krzyzewski said. "He was in the best shape and could play the longest. I thought I worked hard when I was a player, and when I watched him work, I thought, 'He would have just killed me.' "

*Born: June 28, 1977, Jersey City, N.J.*

*"I thought I worked hard when I was a player, and when I watched him work, I thought, 'He would have just killed me.'"*

— Mike Krzyzewski

## CAREER STATS

**Career Pts: 1,731**  **Scoring Avg: 12.4**  **Assists: 7.7**  **Field Goal %: .410**  **TOURNAMENT PLAY:** **NCAA: 1990, 1991, 1992, 1993 (18-2)**  **NCAA Final Four: 1990, 1991, 1992**  **NCAA Champion: 1991, 1992**

**AWARDS AND ACHIEVEMENTS** **Consensus All-American, 1993**  **NABC All-American, 1992**
**NCAA Tournament Most Outstanding Player, 1992**

**Height/Weight: 6-1/165**  **High School: St. Anthony's High, Jersey City**  **College: Duke University, 1989-1993**

# 29 Larry JOHNSON

## CAREER STATS

Career Pts: **1,617**

Scoring Avg: **21.6**

Rebounding Avg: **11.2**

Field Goal %: **.643**

## TOURNAMENT PLAY
NCAA: 1990, 1991

NCAA Final Four: 1990, 1991

NCAA Champion: 1990

## AWARDS AND ACHIEVEMENTS
Robertson Trophy, Naismith Award, Wooden Award, 1991

Consensus All-American, 1991

Consensus All-American, 1990

*Born: March 14, 1969, Dallas*

## "The most unselfish star I've coached."

—Jerry Tarkanian

For Jerry Tarkanian, the toughest part of coaching Larry Johnson was getting him to share less with his UNLV teammates. Johnson wasn't hungry for attention, which meant he wasn't greedy about shots. Ordinarily, that is a wonderful quality for a player, but a guy with Johnson's gifts would have had a hard time finding a way to shoot too often.

Tarkanian called Johnson "the most unselfish star I've coached." In two seasons with the Rebels, Johnson attempted fewer than 13 shots per game. That included the 1990 NCAA championship blowout of Duke, when even the team manager could have launched some extra shots without hurting the cause. Johnson dictated the course of the game with 11 rebounds and four steals, but he shot 8-of-12 for 22 points. He ceded the Most Outstanding Player award to Anderson Hunt, who scored 29 on a hot shooting night.

Johnson's unassuming personality made him a champion as much as his incredible strength and skill. Enough of a power forward to rank among the NCAA's top 15 rebounders, he shot comfortably from 3-point range.

Originally signed to stay home in Dallas and attend SMU, Johnson spent two years at a junior college after his admissions test was questioned. He was asked to retake the test and was about to agree when his high school coach convinced him it was his integrity that was being challenged.

He could have been a prime draft choice if he'd left UNLV following the national championship but remained committed to improving and the challenge of becoming the first team since the UCLA dynasty to repeat as champion. With Johnson accompanied by veterans Hunt, Stacey Augmon and Greg Anthony, the Rebels constructed one of the most overwhelming regular seasons.

They stormed into the Final Four with a 34-0 record and an average margin of 27 points. UNLV met Duke in the semifinals, but this time could not overcome a more mature and confident group of Blue Devils, who got the winning points in the final minute on two Christian Laettner free throws. The Rebels had a last chance to win or tie. Johnson caught the ball on the right wing and passed to Hunt, who let fly with a 3-point attempt. It proved to be a missed opportunity for UNLV—literally.

**Height/Weight:** 6-7/235    **High School:** Skyline High, Dallas    **College:** Odessa (Tex.) College—University of Nevada, Las Vegas 1989-1991

# 30 Chris MULLIN

Just as basketball was rising above the rim for good, Chris Mullin reminded spectators of the beauty that can occur close to the floor. He rarely dunked. He almost never soared toward the ceiling to reject a shot. He got the slightest elevation on his jump shot. Those who appreciated the game considered him as exciting as any player.

Mullin won or shared the Big East player of the year trophy three times. A local kid from Brooklyn, he was the central piece of perhaps the greatest St. John's team, which included future pros Mark Jackson, Bill Wennington and Walter Berry. In such company, there never was a doubt the team revolved around Mullin. He was such an accomplished passer, none of his teammates minded him touching the ball so often.

When THE SPORTING NEWS profiled Mullin during his dazzling senior season, rival coach Gary Williams of Boston College said he would encourage Mullin to shoot more to disrupt the team's seamless chemistry. "It's obvious he figured out that the way to be a great player is to be a great passer," Williams said. "You put two men on him, and he'll just dump it to the open man for a layup."

It wasn't as though Mullin wasted shots. He often fired long-range jumpers but still hit 58 percent as a sophomore and 57 percent as a junior. "There aren't many guys I would just immediately jump out and say 'automatic' when he squared to shoot the basketball," said ESPN basketball analyst Dick Vitale.

In Mullin's final season, St. John's reached the No. 1 ranking and carried coach Lou Carnesecca to his only Final Four. Mullin led all NCAA Tournament players in scoring.

Mullin did not have great jumping ability or quick feet, but he learned always to be in proper position to handle defensive assignments and to use his ball skills to disarm more athletic defenders. "Maybe once in a lifetime you get one like him," Carnesecca said during Mullin's last season. Mullin averaged 4.3 assists along with his 19.8 points, and St. John's won the Big East championship over favored Georgetown. It was a beautiful thing to watch.

*Born: July 30, 1963, New York*

*"There aren't many guys I would just immediately jump out and say 'automatic' when he squared to shoot the basketball."*

—ESPN basketball analyst Dick Vitale

### CAREER STATS

Career Pts: **2,440**

Scoring Avg: **19.5**

Rebounding Avg: **4.1**

Field Goal %: **.550**

### TOURNAMENT PLAY
NCAA: 1982, 1983, 1984, 1985 (6-4)

NCAA Final Four: 1985

### AWARDS AND ACHIEVEMENTS
Robertson Trophy, Wooden Award, 1985

Consensus All-American, 1985

UPI All-American, 1984

Height/Weight: **6-6/210**   High School: **Xaverian High, Brooklyn, N.Y.**   College: **St. John's University, 1981-1985**

# 31 Darrell GRIFFITH

H is entrance into the Louisville program might as well have come through the roof of Freedom Hall. With the dunk at the height of its importance and appeal, Darrell Griffith's jumping ability was of foremost importance. Measurement of his vertical leap—48 inches, they said—was cited more frequently than his scoring average.

In his final game with the Cardinals, four years later, Griffith did not dunk once. He scored 23 of his team's 59 points with long-distance shots, pull-up jumpers and layups. Louisville defeated UCLA for the NCAA championship.

Opponents who had heard so much about his extraordinary athletic ability often were surprised by Griffith's lethal jump shot—and unsettled by their inability to stop it. Griffith leaped so high before releasing an attempt that few defenders could climb high enough to bother him.

Griffith had been a high school sensation in Louisville, winning a state championship at Male High. Upon joining the Cardinals, he was expected to turn a Final Four program into a national champion. It took a little while for that to develop. Griffith was mostly a reserve his first year and thought about leaving school for the NBA after both his sophomore and junior seasons, which were affected by a balky relationship with coach Denny Crum. Crum wanted Griffith to be more disciplined with the basketball and alert on defense. In an NCAA Tournament loss to Arkansas that closed the 1979 season, Griffith was outplayed by the Razorbacks' Sidney Moncrief and was benched down the stretch.

Griffith at last recognized the challenge and worked to address criticism of his play. Midway through Griffith's senior year, Crum told *Basketball Weekly*, "It's a lot harder for a guard to be a dominant player like a 6-9 forward or a 7-0 center, but if a guard can dominate, he is the one. He does everything you ask a player at his position to do."

Griffith averaged 5.2 assists and 5.4 rebounds in the 1980 tournament. Opposing wings such as Kansas State's Rolando Blackman, LSU's Howard Carter and UCLA's Michael Holton struggled to get open shots against him. He averaged 28.5 points in two Final Four games. He passed, rebounded, defended and scored. He didn't dunk. Big deal.

*Born: June 16, 1958, Louisville*

72 Legends of College Basketball

*Opponents who had heard so much about his extraordinary athletic ability often were surprised by Griffith's lethal jump shot—and unsettled by their inability to stop it.*

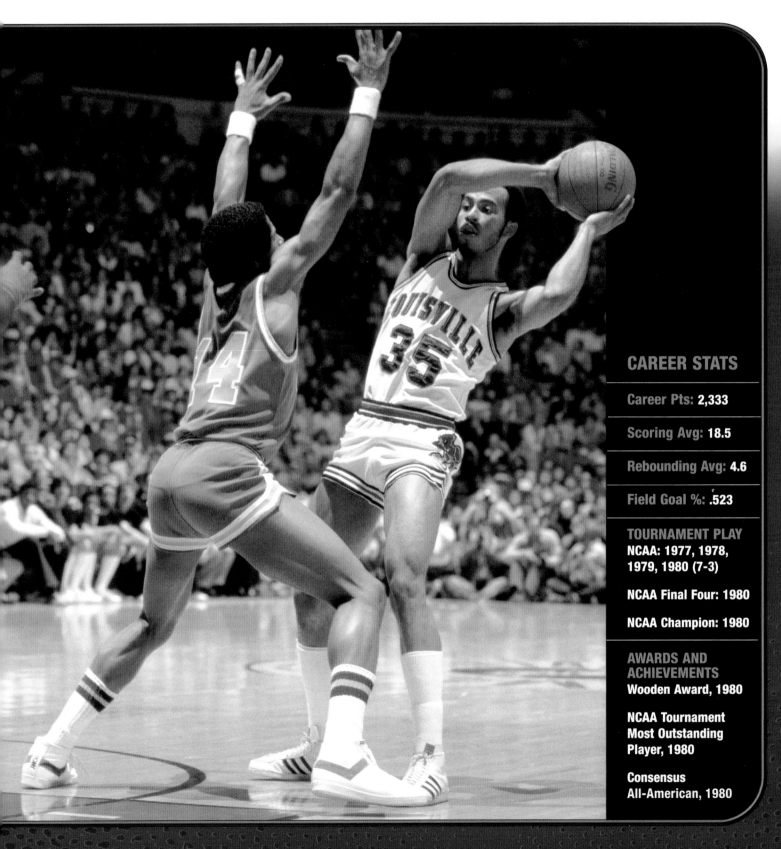

**CAREER STATS**

Career Pts: **2,333**

Scoring Avg: **18.5**

Rebounding Avg: **4.6**

Field Goal %: **.523**

**TOURNAMENT PLAY**
NCAA: 1977, 1978, 1979, 1980 (7-3)

NCAA Final Four: 1980

NCAA Champion: 1980

**AWARDS AND ACHIEVEMENTS**
Wooden Award, 1980

NCAA Tournament Most Outstanding Player, 1980

Consensus All-American, 1980

*Height/Weight: 6-4/195     High School: Male High, Louisville     College: University of Louisville, 1976-1980*

# 32 Scott MAY

On the perfect team, Scott May was the ideal player. He was rugged, disciplined, unselfish and efficient—precisely the qualities that made Indiana's 1976 Hoosiers the greatest college team.

Indiana went through 32 games in 1975-76 without a loss, winning the Big Ten Conference and NCAA championships. May was joined in the lineup by guards Quinn Buckner and Bobby Wilkerson, forward Tom Abernethy and center Kent Benson. Each was capable enough to enjoy an extended NBA career, but the convergence of their efforts created a force exceeding their individual abilities.

"It was a team in maybe just a little different class than all the other teams," May later said. "Everyone knew their roles, and there was no pressure of anyone breaking into the lineup. That was set from day one."

Though it was difficult to stand out in such accomplished company, May became the Hoosiers' scoring star. He preferred not to be known simply for producing points and wanted it to be understood he also rebounded, passed and defended. On such a complete team, the absence of these qualities would have been glaring, but then, so was his 23.5 scoring average as a senior. It was the highest for any player who competed for coach Bob Knight at Indiana.

Deftly using screens set by Abernethy and Benson, May worked to free himself from defenders. Buckner and Wilkerson got May the ball, and he was a lethal mid-range shooter. In the Holiday Festival title game in December 1975, St. John's coach Lou Carnesecca alternated defenders to keep them fresh against May. He still managed 29 points.

May played on the losing side only six times in three seasons. He was so important to Indiana that when he broke his arm late in the 1974-75 season, an unbeaten Hoosiers team fell to Kentucky in the NCAA Tournament. They compensated for that disappointment with their flawless follow-up the following year.

May was a football star in high school and had the opportunity to play wide receiver for several Big Ten powers. He believed he was a basketball player first and chose to become a small forward for Knight's Hoosiers. It turned out to be the perfect choice.

## CAREER STATS

Career Pts: **1,593**    Scoring Avg: **17.7**    Rebounding Avg: **6.6**
Field Goal %: **.513**    TOURNAMENT PLAY: NCAA: **1975, 1976 (7-1)**
NCAA Final Four: **1976**    NCAA Champion: **1976**
AWARDS AND ACHIEVEMENTS: **Naismith Award, 1976**
Consensus All-American, **1976**    Consensus All-American, **1975**

*Born: April 23, 1953 Sandusky, Ohio    Height/Weight: 6-7/218    High School: Sandusky High    College: Indiana University, 1973-1976*

# 33

# Sidney WICKS

**W**hen Sidney Wicks played his first varsity season at UCLA in 1969, box scores did not always reveal the precise number of minutes played by each participant in a game. Wicks did not need accounting to recognize he wasn't playing as much as he wanted.

He frequently approached Bruins coach John Wooden and argued he was better than the forwards playing ahead of him. Wooden agreed. "It's a shame you're letting them beat you out," he said.

"It took him a whole year to learn how to play the team game," Wooden said. "If he's not working well with the team, he's not a star player. He's just potentially a star player."

Though he had power, skill and leaping ability, Wicks averaged 7.5 points as a sophomore for UCLA's 1969 national champions. In the title-game victory over Purdue—a game in which playing time was recorded—he was on the floor for six minutes. But he was "coming along," according to Wooden.

As a junior, Wicks moved into the lineup and became the Bruins' top scorer (18.6) and rebounder (11.9) and an All-American. Wicks was right about his talent. The completion of Lew Alcindor's career left the team without a true big man, so Wooden shifted the team back to the high-post offense by positioning center Steve Patterson near the foul line and relied on Wicks to secure the baseline.

Despite Wooden's emphasis on team function, he ran isolation plays for Wicks. "His junior and senior years, Sidney was the best college forward in the country," Wooden said. "He was a great competitor. He wasn't a great free-throw shooter, but he was in the clutch. I'd want Sidney up there when it counted."

Wicks became the college player of the year as a senior, averaging 21.3 points. But the unselfish play Wooden wanted from him was evident throughout the NCAA Tournament. He scored more than 20 points just once in four games. In the championship game against Villanova, which UCLA won 68-62, he shot only seven times and scored seven points while center Patterson starred for the Bruins with 29 points on 13-of-18 shooting. Wicks played all 40 minutes. He passed for seven assists.

## CAREER STATS

**Career Pts:** 1,423    **Scoring Avg:** 15.8    **Rebounding Avg:** 9.9    **Field Goal %:** .511
**TOURNAMENT PLAY:**    NCAA: 1969, 1970, 1971 (12-0)    NCAA Final Four: 1969, 1970, 1971
**NCAA Champion:** 1969, 1970, 1971
**AWARDS AND ACHIEVEMENTS:** Robertson Trophy, 1971
**NCAA Tournament Most Outstanding Player, 1970**
**Consensus All-American, 1971**    **U.S. Basketball Writers All-American, 1970**

**Born:** Sept. 19, 1949, Los Angeles    **Height/Weight:** 6-8/225    **High School:** Hamilton High, Los Angeles    **College:** UCLA, 1968-1971

# 34 Bob LANIER

The 1970 Final Four proceeded without Bob Lanier. He was the nation's best big man and delivered his team to the verge of a national championship, but when St. Bonaventure made it to Maryland's Cole Field House for the season's ultimate weekend, Lanier was indisposed.

There had been this small collision during the Bonnies' regional final victory over Villanova. It seemed innocent enough when Wildcats guard Chris Ford inadvertently bumped Lanier's right leg, but Lanier's knee was injured. He would not play in another game at St. Bonaventure, which performed valiantly without him but fell to Jacksonville in the national semifinals.

Bonnies fans still view this as a lost opportunity to dethrone perennial champion UCLA. Their team had lost once in 26 games and won three prior NCAA Tournament games by double-figure margins—when they had Lanier.

He was a big man, not just a tall man, with a wide torso, a sturdy trunk and huge feet. Though he could bully around the goal, he developed a sweet 15-foot jumper that prevented opponents from suffocating him with defenders along the baseline. Lanier had a power hook that lacked the delicate choreography that made Lew Alcindor's so picturesque; Lanier's dared anyone to get in the way.

"I remember so many games when he was double- and triple-teamed, and the elbows and sulphurous words were flying around his shoulders. I never saw him flustered or upset," wrote Cy Kritzer, who covered Lanier's Bonnies for the *Buffalo Evening News.* "If there was no way to shoot, he set up an easy shot for one of his teammates or went outside."

Lanier averaged 29.1 points and 16 rebounds as a senior at St. Bonaventure. He scored 50 at Madison Square Garden in the Holiday Festival championship game in December 1969, hitting 18 of his 22 floor attempts and outgunning Purdue's great Rick Mount by 31 points in a huge Bonnies victory. In three seasons, Lanier's teams faced rival Niagara and All-American scoring machine Calvin Murphy six times. St. Bonaventure won them all.

The last was part of 12-game winning streak St. Bonaventure carried into the 1970 NCAA East Region final against Villanova. The 13th game in that run proved to be unlucky.

*Born: Sept. 10, 1948, Buffalo*

*"I never saw him flustered or upset."*

— Writer Cy Kritzer

## CAREER STATS

**Career Pts: 2,067**

**Scoring Avg: 27.6**

**Rebounding Avg: 15.7**

**Field Goal %: .576**

**TOURNAMENT PLAY**
**NCAA: 1968, 1970 (4-1)**

**NCAA Final Four: 1970 (injured)**

**AWARDS AND ACHIEVEMENTS**
**Consensus All-American, 1970**

**Converse All-American, 1969**

*Height/Weight: 6-11/260     High School: Bennett High, Buffalo     College: St. Bonaventure University, 1967-1970*

# 35 Steve ALFORD

Through the course of the 1986-87 season, the first in which the 3-point shot was in force for all of college basketball, few might have imagined how important it would become to the game. And perhaps no one realized there might never be a finer long-ball shooter than Indiana's Steve Alford.

He hit 3-point shots consistently—and he hit them under pressure. With more than 64,000 watching at the Superdome in New Orleans, Alford sank all but three of his 10 attempts and propelled Indiana to a 74-73 victory over Syracuse in the NCAA championship game.

Alford connected on 53 percent of his 3-pointers as a senior, making 107-of-202 from long range, a level of accuracy and productivity nearly unmatched since. He didn't have to change his style or stray outside coach Bob Knight's motion offense. This was the ideal confluence of a coach's system, a player's gifts and a well-timed rule change.

Alford was born the son of a coach, Sam Alford, so he had a natural appreciation for the genius of Knight's attack. "It was a great system, and it helped my game," Alford said. "I thought it was made for me."

Growing up in Indiana, Alford was so intent on playing for Knight he committed to join the Hoosiers before his junior year at New Castle High. Although there were some turbulent moments between the two—"There were some unbelievable practices," Alford said— Knight so abhorred the thought of removing his shooting star from a game Alford averaged at least 36 minutes in each of his four seasons. He did not rest in the 1987 championship game.

Alford was more than a shooter. In the NCAA championship game, he passed for five assists. He was the school's career steals leader until guard Dane Fife passed him during the 2001-02 season. But when the Hoosiers needed points at the 1987 Final Four, Alford torched UNLV for 33 and Syracuse for 23. He'd curl behind a screen set by Darryl Thomas, Dean Garrett or Steve Eyl and cut loose his air-tight jump shot with a flick of his wrist.

"My shooting is probably what people will remember the most," Alford said, "and probably rightfully so."

*Born: Nov. 23, 1964  Franklin, Ind.*

## "My shooting is probably what people will remember the most and probably rightfully so."

—Steve Alford

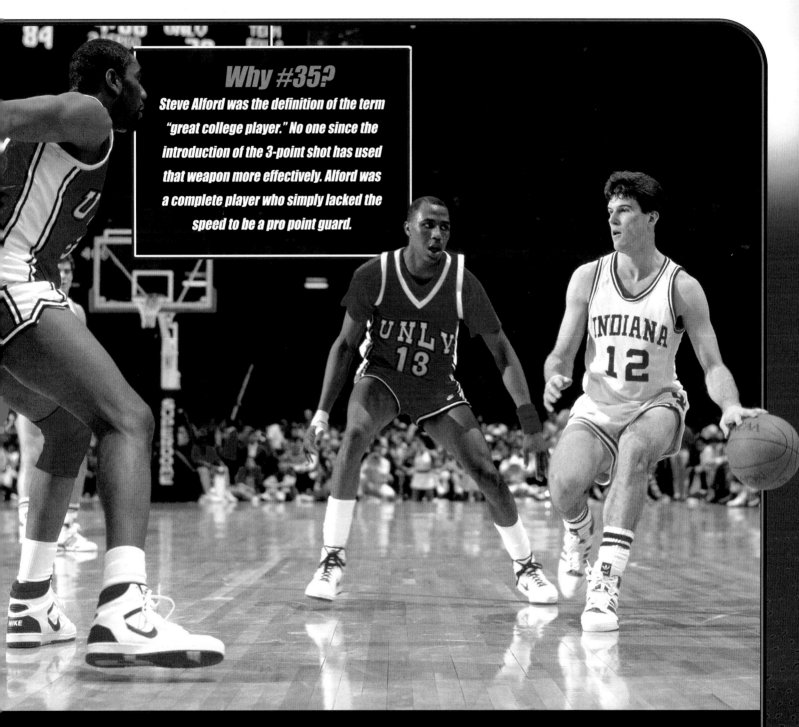

### Why #35?

Steve Alford was the definition of the term "great college player." No one since the introduction of the 3-point shot has used that weapon more effectively. Alford was a complete player who simply lacked the speed to be a pro point guard.

## CAREER STATS

Career Pts: **2,438**    Scoring Avg: **19.5**    3-Point %: **.530**    Field Goal %: **.533**

TOURNAMENT PLAY:  NCAA: 1984, 1986, 1987  (8-2)    NCAA Final Four: 1987    NCAA Champion: 1987    NIT: 1985

AWARDS AND ACHIEVEMENTS Consensus All-American, 1987    Consensus All-American, 1986

Height/Weight: *6-2/183*    High School: *New Castle High, Ind.*    College: *Indiana University, 1983-1987*

# 36 Bob PETTIT

In the land where football was king, at a time when Kentucky was the baron of Southeastern Conference basketball, it took a special player to boost any competitor to parity with the Wildcats. Bob Pettit was born almost for this specific purpose, because he was born in Baton Rouge.

Pettit's decision to stay close to home for college swung the balance of SEC power to LSU as Kentucky also was dealing with the pain of its point-shaving scandal. However, he chose LSU because he doubted his ability to succeed at a school where basketball was revered.

Pettit improved rapidly as a member of the freshman team and was an immediate success in 1951-52, his first varsity season. He was almost dangerously lean, but his agility and aggression made him a fearsome rebounder. He was alert enough to read where potential rebounds were headed and used his long arms and leaping ability to reach the ball before it neared the grasp of opponents.

As a sophomore, Pettit hinted at his promise with 25 points—that bested Kentucky star Cliff Hagan—in a 44-43 SEC Tournament loss to the Wildcats. Not many picked up the clue. Basketball remained an afterthought for a majority of Tigers fans.

LSU was harder to ignore the following year. With Kentucky's program shut down by the NCAA, the Tigers compiled an unbeaten conference season. They entered the NCAA Tournament with a 20-1 record and advanced to the Final Four. Pettit averaged 30.5 points in four games.

As a senior, he used his baseline touch and flawless hook shot to lift that average to 31.4 points and carry it through the season, in which the Tigers shared the SEC title with Kentucky—both with perfect marks—and again reached the NCAAs. Pettit scored 60 in one game, the first SEC player to reach that mark.

It was Pettit's misfortune to set scoring records at LSU, where guard Pete Maravich later would play and nearly lap his career points total twice. But Pettit's number was the first retired for any LSU athlete. He even has a street named for him near the campus. For a basketball player in Baton Rouge, that is twice the honor.

*Born: Feb. 12, 1932, Baton Rouge, La.*

*He was almost dangerously lean, but his agility and aggression made him a fearsome rebounder.*

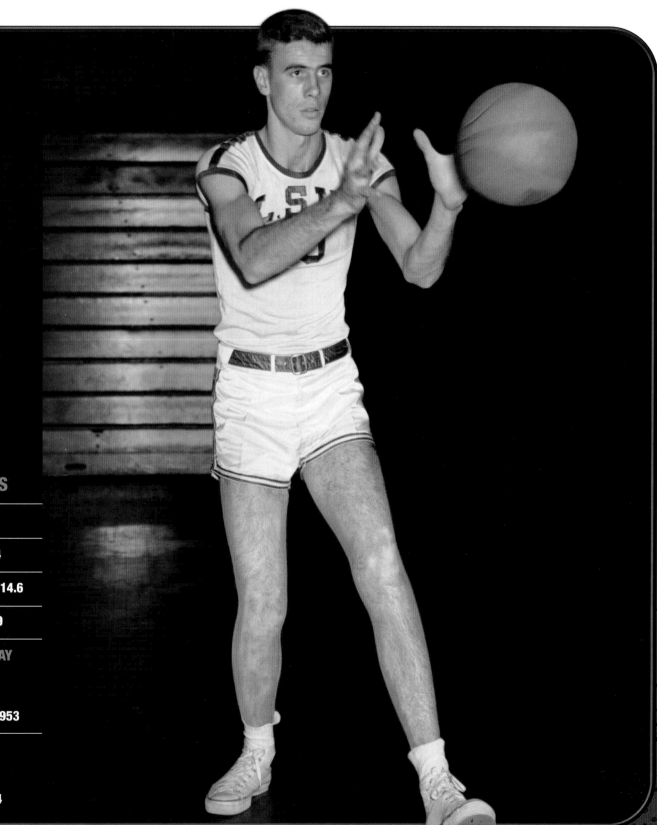

## CAREER STATS

**Career Pts: 1,893**

**Scoring Avg: 27.4**

**Rebounding Avg: 14.6**

**Field Goal %: .469**

**TOURNAMENT PLAY**
**NCAA: 1953, 1954 (2-2)**

**NCAA Final Four: 1953**

**AWARDS AND ACHIEVEMENTS**
**Consensus All-American, 1954**

*Height/Weight: 6-9/215    High School: Baton Rouge High    College: Louisiana State University, 1951-1954*

# 37 Jason WILLIAMS

To appreciate how imposing Jason Williams was during his Duke career, the best people to ask were coaches. They presented a clear answer by choosing him over teammate Shane Battier for the 2001 National Association of Basketball Coaches player of the year award. All the coaches would have loved to work with Battier, who earned nearly every other major trophy. None wanted to contend with Williams.

Skip Prosser took over the Wake Forest program when Williams was in his final season and had to deal with him only three times. "There are like a million concerns with him," Prosser said. Larry Shyatt, who coached Clemson against Williams through seven agonizing defeats, said defending him nearly was a lost cause. "I've never seen anyone who could take credit for stopping Jason Williams," Shyatt said.

The Blue Devils finished the regular season ranked No. 1 in the polls in each of Williams' three seasons. As a sophomore, he was the leading scorer for their national championship team, averaging 21.6 for the season and 25.7 in NCAA Tournament games. He could be streaky as a 3-point shooter. He shot 3-of-20 in the 2001 Final Four after hitting 14-of-36 in victories over Missouri, UCLA and Southern California that carried the Blue Devils that far. His ability to burst past defenders and score in the lane rarely abandoned him.

Because he was recruited to be the Devils' point guard, it took a while for Williams to develop into a scoring force. He was handed the responsibility of operating the Duke attack and involving his teammates. He attempted more than 15 shots only six times in 34 games as a freshman. In the last 64 games of his career, he did it 35 times.

"He really defies a position," said Mike Krzyzewski, Williams' coach at Duke. "He certainly could be a flamboyant passer and the point guard someone might want, and he also was a very explosive scorer. He could just ring up points in a short amount of time. Once he got into that mindset, there haven't been many guys better than him anywhere."

**Born:** Sept. 10, 1981, Plainfield, N.J.    **Height/Weight:** 6-2/195    **High School:** St. Joseph's High, Metuchen, N.J.

*"I've never seen anyone who could take credit for stopping Jason Williams."*

—Larry Shyatt

**CAREER STATS**

Career Pts: **2,079**

Scoring Avg: **19.3**

Assists: **6.0**

3-Point %: **.393**

**TOURNAMENT PLAY**
NCAA: 2000, 2001, 2002 (10-2)

NCAA Final Four: 2001

NCAA Champion: 2001

**AWARDS AND ACHIEVEMENTS**
Robertson Trophy, Naismith Award, Wooden Award, 2002

NABC Player of the Year, 2001

Consensus All-American, 2002

Consensus All-American 2001

*College: Duke University, 1999-2002*

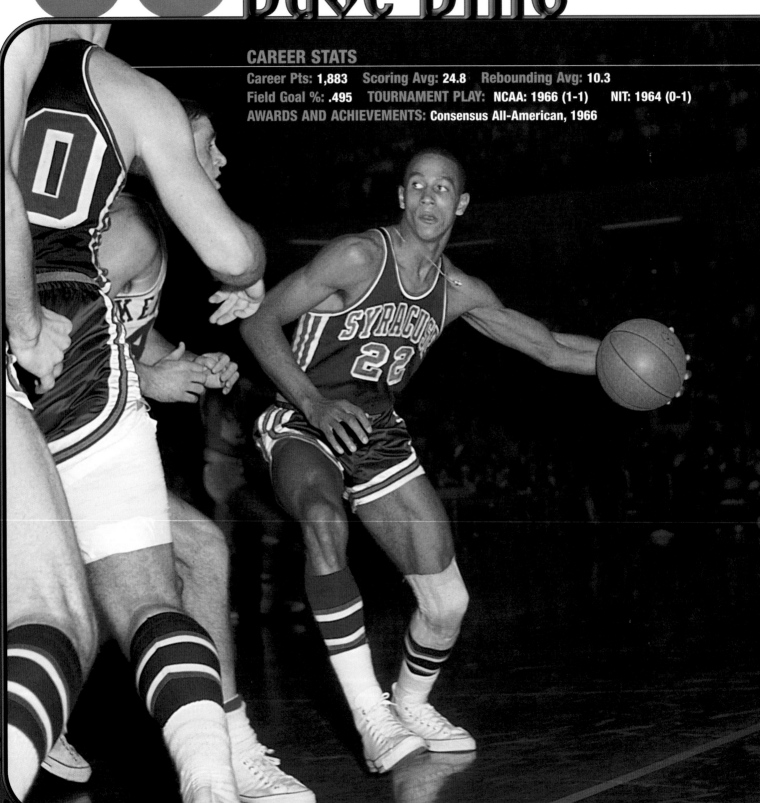

# 38 Dave BING

**CAREER STATS**

Career Pts: **1,883**    Scoring Avg: **24.8**    Rebounding Avg: **10.3**

Field Goal %: **.495**    TOURNAMENT PLAY:  NCAA: **1966 (1-1)**    NIT: **1964 (0-1)**

AWARDS AND ACHIEVEMENTS: **Consensus All-American, 1966**

*Born: Nov. 24, 1943, Washington, D.C.    Height/Weight: 6-3/180    High School: Spingarn High, Washington*

## "He wasn't just good in his time. He would have been good in any time."
### —Jim Boeheim

Before enrolling at Syracuse to pursue his education and playing career, Jim Boeheim had been an all-state guard in central New York. He figured he could handle himself at the college level. Then, after arriving on campus, he got a look at Dave Bing.

"I came into the gym and said, 'I'm in the wrong place,' " Boeheim said. "He was a modern player. He had a modern game. He dunked it over guys, put it behind his back, had great speed and great quickness. He was ahead of his time."

A 6-3 guard, Bing came to Syracuse from the fertile basketball playgrounds of Washington and helped establish a genuine fervor for the sport that still helps Orange fans endure the city's snowy winters. He didn't know exactly what to expect from those winters when he was recruited; the program's coaches timed his recruiting visit to coincide with the (late) arrival of spring.

The basketball program Bing entered was obviously lifeless. The year before he had arrived, the Orangemen finished 2-22. In his final season, they won 22 of their 28 games, led the nation in scoring with 99 points per game and reached the NCAA Tournament for only the second time in their history.

Bing's speed and jumping ability nearly were unprecedented for a guard. Although he was a proficient jump shooter, he did not have to rely entirely upon that skill. He employed his athletic ability with a high degree of efficiency, a sense of when he needed to be spectacular and when to make his teammates' abilities the issue.

The leadership skills that later made Bing a successful businessman were apparent then. Boeheim, who was his backcourt mate and roommate, called Bing "the best leader I've ever been around."

Through three decades as the Syracuse coach, through 21 NCAA Tournaments and more than 600 victories, Boeheim worked with dozens of terrific players. He continues to search for someone as good as Bing.

"He's still the best player that ever played at Syracuse. It's not even close," Boeheim said. "We've had some great players, but not anybody like him. He wasn't just good in his time. He would have been good in any time."

*College: Syracuse University, 1963-1966*

# 39 Ralph SAMPSON

He towered over everyone in the game. This was Ralph Sampson's singular talent. In an age when gifted big men almost became routine—Patrick Ewing, Akeem Olajuwon, Keith Lee—Sampson stood above them all.

His scoring statistics never were spectacular. Sampson never attempted more than 12.5 shots per game during his career and never averaged 20 points. In 132 games, he reached the 40-point mark once.

However, the one number—or sequence of numbers—that mattered with Sampson was 7-4. There never had been a player of consequence who stood so tall. Sampson not only had astonishing size, he had grace and agility. So much seemed possible for Virginia when he was in the game. So much seemed impossible for opponents.

"He presented tremendous problems. Teams really struggled, couldn't get the ball inside, and they tried to do everything from the perimeter," said Dick Vitale, college basketball analyst for the ESPN television network. "Many times, you cannot determine how good a player is just on stats. Some guys bring a certain presence that you need to consider in measuring their value."

Sampson was a tremendous rebounder, ranking fourth among players in the modern era with 1,511. The NCAA did not record blocked shots as an official statistic when Sampson played, but Virginia did, and he swatted down an average of 3.5 per game.

In each of his final three seasons, the Cavaliers finished first in the Atlantic Coast Conference regular season. In December 1982, he outdueled Ewing in one of the most widely publicized games ever. Sampson outscored, outrebounded and outblocked Ewing and threw a shattering windmill slam in Ewing's face. No. 1-ranked Virginia earned a 68-63 victory over No. 3 Georgetown.

Where Sampson and Virginia came up short was in the NCAA Tournament. They reached the Final Four once, but dropped a lopsided game in the 1981 national semifinals to a North Carolina team they had swept during the regular season.

"They didn't win a national title, but that isn't always an indicator of how great a player is," Vitale said. "With any Goliath, any superstar, you get maligned when you don't bring home the gold. On the collegiate level, he was a dominant force."

**Born: July 7, 1960, Harrisonburg, Va.**

*"He presented tremendous problems. Teams really struggled, couldn't get the ball inside, and they tried to do everything from the perimeter."*

— Dick Vitale

## Why #39?

*Ralph Sampson was a three-time player of the year, but in retrospect those honors have too much of a you-had-to-be-there quality. His ability to affect a game was unquestioned, but there were times he did not deliver in the clutch.*

## CAREER STATS

Career Pts: **2,228**

Scoring Avg: **16.9**

Rebounding Avg: **11.4**

Field Goal %: **.568**

### TOURNAMENT PLAY
NCAA: 1981, 1982, 1983, (6-3)

NCAA: Final Four, 1981

NIT Champion: 1980

### AWARDS AND ACHIEVEMENTS
Robertson Trophy, Naismith Award, Wooden Award, 1983

Robertson Trophy, Naismith Award, Wooden Award, 1982

Robertson Trophy, Naismith Award, 1981

Consensus All-American, 1983

Consensus All-American, 1982

Consensus All-American, 1981

NIT Most Valuable Player, 1980

Height/Weight: **7-4/230**    High School: **Harrisonburg High**    College: **University of Virginia, 1979-1983**

# 40 Bob COUSY

If he were an artist, he would have been classified avant-garde: behind-the-back dribbles, over-the-shoulder passes, twisting layups glancing off the board at curious angles and falling through the rim. Bob Cousy did what be believed would help Holy Cross to win games. If changing direction by bouncing the ball between his legs worked, it didn't matter others perceived this maneuver to be "hot-dogging." Let them try to stop it.

Cousy played in a hunched style that always made him appear smaller than he was. He seemed to focus exclusively on controlling the ball, but his eyes noted and his mind processed every development on the court. His dexterity made his tricks possible, but his vision turned them into legitimate basketball plays.

Fans loved the Cousy style. He routinely drew capacity crowds, but his flair was disdained by some traditionalists—including his coach, Alvin "Doggie" Julian. Cousy as a freshman was an important part of the rotation on the 1947 NCAA championship team, but the player-coach relationship deteriorated the next year. When Cousy missed a practice because of car problems, he was benched for a game against Loyola of Chicago.

Holy Cross built a double-digit lead, but when the Crusaders began squandering it—and with shouts of "We want Cousy" ringing from the audience—Julian sent him into the game. Cousy scored 12 points in the final five minutes, and the Crusaders won by 16. Cousy eventually won over Julian, who called him "amazing" during Cousy's All-American senior season. Cousy averaged 19.4 points and led Holy Cross back to the NCAA Tournament.

Perhaps his most unusual achievement came in his challenging junior year. As the Crusaders rebuilt toward a 19-8 finish, Cousy was named MVP at the Sugar Bowl tournament over Kentucky's Alex Groza and Ralph Beard and Ed Macauley of St. Louis—even though Holy Cross lost both its games.

"I consider Cousy the trickiest ball player I've ever seen," Kentucky coach Adolph Rupp once said. "He is a basketball quarterback. He has a quick change of pace that makes him ever dangerous. He has all the shots and will go down in history as one of the greatest basketball players of all time."

## CAREER STATS

**Career Pts: 1,775**  **Scoring Avg: 15.2**
**TOURNAMENT PLAY:** NCAA: 1947, 1948, 1950 (4-2)   **NCAA Final Four:** 1947, 1948   **NCAA Champion:** 1947
**AWARDS AND ACHIEVEMENTS:** Consensus All-American, 1950

**Born:** Aug. 9, 1928, New York   **Height/Weight:** 6-1/175   **High School:** Andrew Jackson, Queens, N.Y   **College:** College of the Holy Cross, 1946-1950

# Walt HAZZARD 41

Althqugh the most obvious source of might through the course of the UCLA dynasty was the frontcourt, where the likes of Lew Alcindor and Bill Walton towered over cowering opponents, the first championship in the Bruins' rampage was delivered by a point guard.

This was one heck of an assist. The Bruins were 30-0 in Walt Hazzard's final season, handily beating Duke in the 1964 NCAA championship game, and the standard of excellence he helped establish resulted in nine more championships during the next 11 years. Hazzard's trek from Philadelphia to Los Angeles demonstrated to Alcindor that he, too, could travel cross-country and discover educational and athletic fulfillment.

Hazzard was a point guard in an era dominated by points guards. In his high school and college career, he never averaged 20 points. He produced an 18.9 scoring average in 1963-64. None of the other four players who were first-team All-Americans in Hazzard's senior year averaged fewer than 24. "In a game dominated by high scoring," wrote UPI sportswriter Art Spander, "Hazzard has turned the arts of passing and dribbling into more of an offensive show than a 30-point-a-game average."

The Harlem Globetrotters provided the inspiration for Hazzard to develop his ball skill. As a child, he watched the great Marques Haynes play and became devoted to emulating those tricks. Though UCLA coach John Wooden had to trim the excesses from that act when Hazzard was a sophomore and the Bruins opened with a 4-7 record, there was enough cleverness left to distract and destabilize opponents. As Hazzard began to feel comfortable with his responsibilities, the Bruins closed with 14 wins in the final 18 games and Wooden's first trip to the Final Four.

With Hazzard and backcourt mate Gail Goodrich leading the attack the next two seasons, Wooden employed a fullcourt zone press that led to utter dominance. Hazzard's quickness enabled him to deflect or steal the ball and his vision and daring transformed those turnovers into passes that preceded Bruins layups.

"I consider him as good a passer—if not the best—as there is in college basketball," Goodrich said. "I had confidence that if I got open, he was going to get me the ball."

## CAREER STATS
**Career Pts: 1,401**  **Scoring Avg: 16.1**  **Rebounding Avg: 5.5**
**Field Goal %: .432**  **TOURNAMENT PLAY: NCAA: 1962, 1963, 1964, (6-2)**
**NCAA Final Four: 1962, 1964**  **NCAA Champion: 1964**
**AWARDS AND ACHIEVEMENTS: Robertson Trophy, 1964**  **NCAA Tournament Most Outstanding Player, 1964**

*Born: April 15, 1942, Philadelphia  Height/Weight: 6-2/188  High School: Overbrook High, Philadelphia  College: UCLA, 1961-1964*

# 42 Clyde LOVELLETTE

Some college coaches simply make pitches to recruits they covet, and some go so far as to make promises. In pursuing center Clyde Lovellette, Kansas coach Phog Allen issued a prophecy. Allen said by becoming a Jayhawk, Lovellette would position himself to win an NCAA championship and Olympic gold medal four years later.

Allen believed everything else was in place save for the ideal big man: Lovellette, a 6-9 wide-body some called "The Great White Whale." Lovellette went to high school in Indiana, where a star player was expected to become a Hoosier, but the prophecy intrigued him enough he instead chose KU.

Joining Bob Kenney, Bill Lienhard and Bill Hougland, Lovellette formed a sort of Fab Four recruiting class. The others were primarily role players willing to sacrifice to pursue a championship. Lovellette was the star to carry them.

Allen convinced Lovellette to learn the hook shot, and a year's worth of work made him proficient with either hand by the time his varsity career began in 1949-50. His was not a sweeping hook, but instead released as quickly as a scorpion's sting. Lovellette increased his scoring output each season and dominated 1951-52—exactly as Allen had predicted.

Averaging 28.4 points, Lovellette became the only player to lead the NCAA in scoring and win the national championship in the same season.

Kansas squeezed through a difficult first-round game against TCU, then won the next three by an average of 18 points. The Jayhawks brought a touch of modernity to the sport; they were the first NCAA champion to top 60 points in every tournament game. Lovellette averaged 35.3. The final part of Allen's prophecy was fulfilled when six players from that team were selected to compete in the 1952 Summer Olympics and claimed the gold medal.

"I don't believe there was any time that came up when anyone said, 'You're scoring too many points,' " Lovellette said. "I had a crew of guys with me that were not selfish. When we get together and talk about the season we had—we don't talk about how good I was; we talk about how good our team was."

## CAREER STATS

**Career Pts: 1,888**

**Scoring Avg: 24.5**

**Rebounding Avg: 10.2**

**Field Goal %: .452**

### TOURNAMENT PLAY
**NCAA: 1952 (4-0)**

**NCAA Final Four: 1952**

**NCAA Champion: 1952**

### AWARDS AND ACHIEVEMENTS
**NCAA Tournament Most Outstanding Player, 1952**

**Consensus All-American, 1952**

**Consensus All-American, 1951**

*Born: Sept 7, 1929, Petersburg, Ind.   Height/Weight: 6-9/240   High School: Garfield (Ind.) High   College: University of Kansas, 1949-1952*

# Ralph BEARD

## 43

is game was speed. Kentucky guard Ralph Beard moved so quickly a sportswriter once suggested the breeze he created on his drives to the goal could give an opponent pneumonia. "I was the quickest guy around," Beard said, more to be illuminating than immodest.

Beard could, in the language of the game, "take my man" any time he wished. That wasn't the way the Wildcats played under Adolph Rupp. There never was a question who was in charge.

"We had 10 plays, could run them with blindfolds on, and it didn't make any difference who made the bucket," Beard said. "Coach Rupp was the star, and we all knew that."

Beard's play at guard was an elemental part of Kentucky's Fabulous Five squad, which dominated in the late 1940s. In his four seasons, the Wildcats compiled a 130-10 record and claimed three postseason championships, including consecutive NCAA titles in 1948 and 1949.

Rupp once suggested Beard was nearly a perfect player. Coaches were enamored of Beard's selfless, energetic style. He never averaged more than 12.5 points in a season, though he was capable of more. As a freshman in 1946, he hit the game-winning free throw with 40 seconds left in the NIT championship game victory over Rhode Island.

"We had so many good players that you had to fight tooth-and-toenail to get any playing time," Beard said. "I was a 17-year-old freshman, and if Coach Rupp had said, 'Ralph, I want you to run through that wall,' I would have said, 'OK, back up and give me some room.' "

He left behind a mountain of achievements at Kentucky, but two years later his legacy was stained when Beard and fellow Wildcats All-American Alex Groza were implicated in the point-shaving scandals that decimated college basketball. Among those who saw Beard play and believed his good name should be restored is former Alabama and Vanderbilt coach C.M. Newton, who played at Kentucky in the early '50s and campaigned for Beard to join him in the Hall of Fame.

Beard did not deny taking money when questioned but later insisted he never acted to influence any game—other than trying to win. He did that as well as any small guard. This should be his legacy.

## CAREER STATS

**Career Pts:** 1,517

**Scoring Avg:** 10.9

**Free Throw %:** .624

## TOURNAMENT PLAY
**NCAA:** 1948, 1949 (6-0)

**NCAA Final Four:** 1948, 1949

**NCAA Champion:** 1948, 1949

**NIT:** 1946, 1947, 1949

**NIT Champion:** 1946

## AWARDS AND ACHIEVEMENTS
**Consensus All-American, 1949**

**Consensus All-American, 1948**

**Consensus All-American, 1947**

**Born:** Dec. 27, 1927, Hardinsburg, Ky.   **Height/Weight:** 5-11/160   **High School:** Male High, Louisville   **College:** University of Kentucky, 1945-1949

# 44 Cliff HAGAN

His trademark shot was not properly trademarked. Whereas Lew Alcindor had a "sky hook," Cliff Hagan just had a hook shot. If his most potent weapon did not have a nickname, however, it certainly had a purpose.

Hagan's expertise with the hook shot made him a high school star for a state championship team in Owensboro and a coveted recruit for his state's university. Kentucky had won two NCAA championships in three seasons before Hagan joined the Wildcats, and he became part of a third by averaging 9.2 points and 8.5 rebounds on a team that went 32-2 and defeated Kansas State in the 1951 NCAA title game. Although he was ill with a throat infection and had an elevated temperature, Hagan entered the game with UK trailing by eight points and sparked a comeback. He made 5-of-6 field goals and scored 10 points in a 68-58 victory.

That turned out to be Hagan's one Final Four appearance. UK lost in a 1952 regional final upset to St. John's despite Hagan's 22 points, after the Wildcats had beaten that same group of Redmen by 41 points in a regular-season game. The following year, the NCAA suspended Kentucky from competition, the fallout from a point-shaving scandal and charges that Wildcats boosters had violated the organization's rules.

What happened during the 1953-54 season might have been more difficult. The Wildcats stormed to a 25-0 record—with an average victory margin of more than 27 points—including a decision over LSU in a one-game playoff to determine the Southeastern Conference champion. However, Kentucky was informed Hagan, guard Frank Ramsey and forward Lou Tsioropoulos were ineligible because the NCAA determined they had accumulated enough credits to graduate. Coach Adolph Rupp refused to play without his three leading scorers. The Helms Foundation declared the Wildcats national champions, anyway, but that distinction faded as surely as the popularity of the hook shot.

Hagan averaged better than 20 points in his final two seasons. He did it primarily with his hook, which he said demanded extraordinary patience to learn the proper feel. It wasn't a glamorous play that inspired sportswriters to conjure fanciful descriptions. It just worked.

*Born: Dec. 9, 1931, Owensboro, Ky.*

*He did it primarily with his hook, which he said demanded extraordinary patience to learn the proper feel. It wasn't a glamorous play that inspired sportswriters to conjure fanciful descriptions. It just worked.*

**CAREER STATS**

Career Pts: **1,475**

Scoring Avg: **19.2**

Rebounding Avg: **13.4**

Field Goal %: **.425**

**TOURNAMENT PLAY**
NCAA: 1951, 1952
(5-1)

NCAA Final Four: 1951

NCAA Champion: 1951

**AWARDS AND ACHIEVEMENTS**
Consensus
All-American, 1954

Consensus
All-American, 1952

*Height/Weight:* 6-4/215    *High School:* Owensboro High    *College:* University of Kentucky, 1950-1954

# 45 Tim DUNCAN

Unfortunately for Tim Duncan, Minneapolis was the site of his most important college game: Wake Forest's battle with Kentucky to determine which would head to the 1996 Final Four. The NBA's Minnesota Timberwolves would select in the league's draft lottery a few months later, and thus many reporters badgered him about his interest in turning professional and ignored the game he was to play.

Because of Duncan's uncommon gifts, his Wake Forest career always seemed to be more about where he was heading (the NBA) than where he was standing (the NCAA). Duncan could have been the NBA's No. 1 overall draft pick following his sophomore and junior seasons. He was committed enough to college, though, to remain at Wake until he'd played four years for the Demon Deacons and graduated from the university.

Duncan started his athletic career as a swimmer in the Virgin Islands and dreamed of competing in the Olympics until a hurricane wiped out the pool he used for training. He began playing basketball more often, grew to a center's height and was noticed by former Wake Forest player Chris King during King's visit to the islands. He convinced coach Dave Odom to recruit Duncan. Odom described Duncan, who'd had little training and competition, as "a piece of clay you can mold."

In four years, Duncan went from scoring no points in his debut against Alaska-Anchorage to averaging 20.8 points, 14.7 rebounds and 3.2 assists as a Wake senior. Though his coaching and competition had been minimal as a teenager, Duncan developed a guard's ballhandling and passing skills, a forward's scoring versatility and a center's body and shot-block timing.

He did not own an NCAA championship, or even a Final Four berth, when he left Wake Forest. He came no closer than that regional final game against Kentucky, when the Wildcats' blistering double-team traps held him to 14 points and produced an easy UK victory. That wasn't enough to chase him out of college basketball and into the NBA's lottery millions. He returned to Wake Forest for one more year as the most versatile big man ever to play college basketball.

*Because of Duncan's uncommon gifts, his Wake Forest career always seemed to be more about where he was heading (the NBA) than where he was standing (the NCAA).*

Born: April 25, 1976, St. Croix, Virgin Islands
Height/Weight: 6-11/245
High School: St. Duncan's Episcopal
College: Wake Forest University, 1993-1997

## CAREER STATS

Career Pts: **2,117**

Scoring Avg: **16.5**

Rebounding Avg: **12.3**

Blocks Avg: **3.8**

### TOURNAMENT PLAY
**NCAA: 1994, 1995, 1996, 1997 (7-4)**

### AWARDS AND ACHIEVEMENTS
**Robertson Trophy, Naismith Award, Wooden Award, 1997**

**Consensus All-American, 1997**

**Consensus All-American, 1996**

# 46 Hank LUISETTI

**W**hat Hank Luisetti would do to a basketball was shocking. He had the nerve to shoot it with only one hand.

Nearly every one of his contemporaries was relying on the two-handed set shot. Luisetti came up with the one-hander when he was still a child and found it worked so well there never was a reason to change to the conventional style. His skill with his technique changed the direction of the sport, helping to make the game more fluid and exciting and marking the first huge step in the evolution of the jump shot. Aside from the elimination of the center jumps that followed every made field goal until 1937, this might have been the most important accelerant to the growth of the game's popularity.

When Luisetti began to excel as a Stanford sophomore, his shooting style shocked others in the college game. Nat Holman, the coach at City College of New York, was quoted as saying the one-hander was "predicated on a prayer" and he would quit the coaching business if forced to teach it.

Then, during Luisetti's junior season, Stanford traveled to New York and faced powerhouse Long Island University at Madison Square Garden. Luisetti scored 15 points in a 45-31 Stanford victory, ending LIU's 43-game winning streak. The following year, Stanford beat both LIU and CCNY on an Eastern swing. Holman was convinced. He praised Luisetti's all-around skill—and his shooting.

He wasn't simply a novelty. Luisetti was a fine defender and passer and an unselfish teammate. But his scoring ability nearly was unprecedented. In his first season, Luisetti averaged 20.3 points. It wasn't unusual for an entire team to finish a game with that total. Against Duquesne in his senior season, he scored 50 points in a 92-27 Stanford victory. In six of the first eight NCAA championship games, the winning team did not hit that mark.

Stanford won Pacific Coast championships in all three of Luisetti's seasons. The end of his career predated the introduction of the NCAA Tournament by a single year, so he did not get to play for a national championship. His consolation? He changed the game so significantly that one day that championship game would rank with the greatest sporting events.

## CAREER STATS

**Career Pts: 1,291**

**Scoring Avg: 16.1**

### AWARDS AND ACHIEVEMENTS

**Helms Foundation Player of the Year, 1938**

**Helms Foundation Player of the Year, 1937**

**Consensus All-American, 1938**

**Consensus All-American, 1937**

**Consensus All-American, 1936**

*Born: June 16, 1916, San Francisco, Calif.   Height/Weight: 6-3/175   High School: Galileo High, San Francisco   College: Stanford University, 1935-1*

96   **Legends of College Basketball**

# Calvin MURPHY 47

H e was something of a novelty when he showed up in Pittsburgh for the Dapper Dan high school all-star game. Calvin Murphy stood 5-9. A few college coaches who watched him average 40.3 points at Connecticut's Norwalk High believed he was worth a scholarship, but others figured his lack of stature would make it difficult for him to compete.

The Dapper Dan game provided an early answer. Playing for a U.S. all-star team against a squad of Pennsylvania's best, Murphy scored 37 points and issued a declaration that coaches would not be able to ignore him when he enrolled at Niagara.

Murphy was electrically quick, a deceptive ballhandler and astounding leaper. He employed what almost could be classified as a two-handed jump shot that twirled off his fingertips and helped account for 33.1 scoring average that ranks fourth in NCAA Division I history.

The ability of one great player to elevate a program is part of what makes basketball attractive for colleges that compete in the highest division. Ordinarily, that player is a big guy—someone like Larry Bird, Artis Gilmore or David Robinson. Murphy could fit into a sock drawer but still became unstoppable as a college guard. He scored 41 points in his first game with the Niagara varsity and averaged 38.2 points that year. He recorded a career-best 68 points against Syracuse, one of the major schools that had recruited him. As a senior, Murphy saw his average drop to 29.4 points, but the Purple Eagles compiled a 21-5 regular-season record that merited the school's only NCAA Tournament appearance. His 35 points against Penn and defensive coaching whiz Dick Harter got Niagara into the NCAA Sweet 16.

Murphy's introduction to college basketball came as a challenge from freshman coach Alex Hannum: If he did not succeed, other small players might not get the chance. When he was introduced in 1993 as a new member of the Naismith Memorial Hall of Fame, Murphy said that when he talking about his career he liked to refer to himself as "the pioneer for the average basketball player. I don't use the word 'small.' " The thing was, Murphy was a lot closer to "small" than he was to "average."

## CAREER STATS

Career Pts: **2,548**

Scoring Avg: **33.1**

Rebounding Avg: **4.0**

Field Goal %: **.438**

### TOURNAMENT PLAY
NCAA: 1970 (1-1)

### AWARDS AND ACHIEVEMENTS
Consensus All-American, 1970

Consensus All-American, 1969

Born: May 9, 1948, Norwalk, Conn.   Height/Weight: 5-9/165   High School: Norwalk High   College: Niagara University, 1967-1970

# 48 Sihugo GREEN

Tracing the evolution of the air game through basketball's history, the chain passes from Vince Carter to Michael Jordan to David Thompson to Julius Erving to Connie Hawkins. It does not stop there. A quiet link in that chain is connected to Duquesne University's Sihugo Green.

In the mid-1950s, when Catholic schools east of the Mississippi became influential by embracing African-American athletes, Green partnered with gifted big man Dick Ricketts to make Duquesne one of the most powerful teams. They played in consecutive National Invitation Tournament championship games, winning the title over Dayton in 1955. Ricketts controlled the baseline and Green took charge just about anywhere.

Green stood 6-3 with a taut upper body and thick, muscular thighs. He wore his socks high on his calves, calling them his "jumping socks." Green did not merely make decorative use of his leaping ability, displaying it for show and intimidation. He used it to deal with taller opponents.

Green was a rebounding force. He averaged 13.6 to go with 22 points per game in 1954-55. In the first round of the 1955 NIT against Louisville, Dukes coach Dudey Moore assigned Green to defend promising 6-8 sophomore Charlie Tyra. In an eight-point Duquesne victory, Tyra managed 16 points to Green's 23. "Si has the speed to match any little man and the jumping ability to match any big man," Moore said then. "His quickness and reaction have never been matched."

Green and Ricketts combined for an astonishing performance in the NIT title game, scoring all of Duquesne's first-half points and the first nine of the second half in a 70-58 triumph. Playing without Ricketts as a senior, Green handled more offensive responsibility and twice topped 40 points. The Dukes were less successful in the regular season but still fought into the NIT quarterfinals.

Though he was not known as an extraordinary outside shooter, Green's speed made it difficult for opponents to cut off his drives. He averaged just short of 10 free-throw attempts per game in his final two seasons. Few could keep him out of the lane. No one could knock him out of the air. Sihugo Green soared. The game of basketball soon followed.

## CAREER STATS

**Career Pts: 1,603    Scoring Avg: 19.8    Rebounding Avg: 11.6    Field Goal %: .422**
**TOURNAMENT PLAY:    NIT: 1954, 1955, 1956    NIT Champion: 1955**
**AWARDS AND ACHIEVEMENTS: Consensus All-American, 1956**
**Consensus All-American, 1955**

**Born: Aug. 20, 1934, Brooklyn, N.Y.    Died: Oct. 4, 1980    Height/Weight: 6-3/185**
**High School: Boys High, Brooklyn    College: Duquesne University, 1953-1956**

# mike BIBBY 49

J ust a freshman as he prepared to make his Final Four debut, Mike Bibby acted so cool he appeared better suited to playing bass in Miles Davis' jazz band than point guard with the Arizona Wildcats. Then, he walked onto the RCA Dome floor in Indianapolis to challenge North Carolina in the national semifinals. He realized where he was, how far he'd come in so little time.

"In the beginning I was a little ... I guess I was nervous for a little bit," Bibby said. In the first 27 minutes against the Tar Heels, he missed eight of his 10 shots. An ordinary player might have stopped shooting, probably should have stopped. This never was a consideration for Bibby.

He finished the second half with six 3-pointers and his 20 points led Arizona into the championship game. There, his ability to drive the basketball and command of the game's flow lifted Arizona over Kentucky to claim his school's first NCAA title.

Bibby would not have been an elite playmaker without his speed and jump shot, but no quality elevated him more than his preternatural sense of calm. Customarily, championship point guards are veterans who lead and make sound decisions. Bibby covered both even though he played his 33rd and 34th college games at the 1997 Final Four.

Bibby was not the Wildcats' primary scorer—that was wing Miles Simon—but he was the reason they became the first team to defeat three No. 1 seeds and the lowest seed (No. 4) to claim a title in the shot-clock era. "He's a sponge," said Lute Olson, Bibby's coach at Arizona. "He just wants to learn every possible thing he can about the game."

Mike Bibby was not the first point guard in his family to claim an NCAA title. His father, Henry, ran the UCLA offense with three championship teams. However, Henry and Virginia Bibby were separated and Mike spent little time with his father. Henry later became coach at Southern California and opposed Mike's Arizona teams several times.

Dealing with this delicate circumstance never seemed to unnerve Mike Bibby. He gently deflected questions about his relationship with his father. He concentrated on the games he was asked to play. The bigger they were, the better he was.

## CAREER STATS

**Career Pts: 1,061**    **Scoring Avg: 15.4**    **Assists Avg: 5.4**    **3-Point %: .390**
**TOURNAMENT PLAY: NCAA: 1997, 1998 (9-1)**    **NCAA Final Four: 1997**
**NCAA Champion: 1997**
**AWARDS AND ACHIEVEMENTS: Consensus All-American, 1998**

**Born: May 13, 1978, Cherry Hill, N.J.**    **Height/Weight: 6-1/180**
**High School: Shadow Mountain High, Phoenix, Ariz.**    **College: University of Arizona, 1996-1998**

# 50 Butch LEE

In conversations about the great New York City guards, the name of Butch Lee is frequently forgotten amid talk of Kenny Anderson, Stephon Marbury, Rod Strickland and Tiny Archibald. Lee did not enjoy the legend-enhancing professional career that can be a prerequisite for inclusion in that sort of discussion, and he played his best ball far removed from the city. Milwaukee, home to Marquette, is not where a New Yorker generally looks for great basketball.

Only one of New York's legendary guards, though, finished his college career with a player of the year trophy and NCAA championship. Lee delivered Marquette to the 1977 national title, outplaying North Carolina's esteemed Phil Ford in the final. A year later, the two split the major honors—the only time that the Naismith, Wooden and Robertson awards were the exclusive property of point guards.

Lee played a New Yorker's game: as flashy as it was substantive, as stylish as it was effective. He was from a different physical mold, with a barrelish build set close to the ground. Though a capable passer, Lee averaged only 2.5 assists in the 1977 NCAA Tournament. But he led Marquette in shot attempts in each game and averaged 19.3 points. It was an approach that worked for the Warriors.

After Lee scored 31 to defeat DePaul in 1977-78, Jerome Whitehead, the Marquette center, expressed appreciation for—not jealousy of—Lee's offensive dominance. "It is nice to have a guy who can take it to them any time he wants," Whitehead told the *Chicago Tribune*. "Butch is so talented. Get the ball to him, and he'll control the tempo. He'll bring up the ball. He'll score. And when they put two and three men around him, he'll dish it off."

Lee was the model of the scoring point guard, but his greatest moment at Marquette was his length-of-court inbounds pass with the Warriors and UNC Charlotte tied and three seconds left in their national semifinal. After the ball was deflected, Whitehead picked it up and squeezed it into the goal. Marquette was in the title game. Lee did not receive an assist for making that pass. He did receive a championship ring.

Born: Dec. 5, 1956, San Juan, Puerto Rico

"It is nice to have a guy who can take it
to them any time he wants."

— Jerome Whitehead

**CAREER STATS**

Career Pts: **1,735**   Scoring Avg: **15.1**   Rebounding Avg: **3.3**   Field Goal %: **.475**

TOURNAMENT PLAY:   NCAA: **1975, 1976, 1977, 1978 (7-3)**, NCAA Final Four: **1977**, NCAA Champion: **1977**

AWARDS AND ACHIEVEMENTS Naismith Award, **1978**      NCAA Tournament Most Outstanding Player, **1977**
Consensus All-American, **1978**

Height/Weight: **6-1/185**   High School: **DeWitt Clinton High, New York City**   College: **Marquette University, 1974-1978**

# 51 Mark AGUIRRE

## CAREER STATS

**Career Pts: 2,182**

**Scoring Avg: 24.5**

**Rebounding Avg: 7.9**

**Field Goal %: .545**

### TOURNAMENT PLAY
**NCAA: 1979, 1980, 1981 (3-3)**

**NCAA Final Four: 1979**

### AWARDS AND ACHIEVEMENTS
**The Sporting News Player Of The Year, 1981**

**Robertson Trophy, Naismith Award, 1980**

**Consensus All-American, 1981**

**Consensus All-American, 1980**

*Born: Dec. 10, 1959, Chicago*

> *"It was exciting to go to practice and know every day you were going to find something out about the game."*
>
> —Mark Aguirre

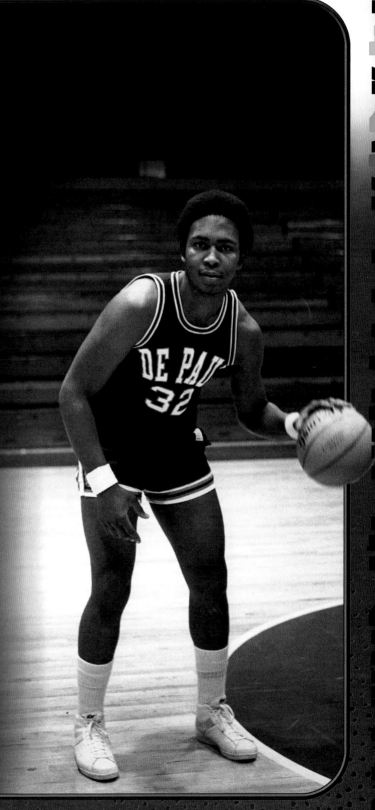

Things were simplest for Mark Aguirre when he was a freshman at DePaul. The college game had other stars to divert the attention: Michigan State's Magic Johnson, Indiana State's Larry Bird. The Blue Demons had experienced seniors to accept the responsibility of running the team. Coach Ray Meyer provided a touch of special treatment when it seemed necessary. Aguirre simply could play.

My, how he played. In 1972-73, freshman eligibility for varsity competition had been restored under NCAA rules, but the organization had not yet seen a freshman exert the enormous influence Aguirre did in his first year at DePaul. He still carried a bit of extra weight, but threw that around in the low post and averaged 24 points. He was the primary ingredient in the Blue Demons' drive to the Final Four, where they lost by a single basket to Indiana State. He joined Bird and Johnson on the all-tournament team.

"I had played with some incredible people growing up in Chicago," Aguirre said. "I felt comfortable when I got to the floor."

From that foundation, Aguirre carried DePaul to a 25-0 start as a sophomore—a perfect record Notre Dame needed double overtime to spoil. As Aguirre's physical condition improved, as his knowledge of how to use his body to draw fouls increased, he became the nation's preeminent player. He was among the top 10 scorers in the nation and won most of the major player of the year awards.

DePaul finished with the No. 1 ranking, but despite superiority during the regular season the Blue Demons were shipped to the NCAA Tournament's West Region. Following a first-round bye, the Blue Demons lost to UCLA. A year later, with Aguirre a junior, the Demons again were ranked No. 1 and again lost their first tournament game. This one, against St. Joseph's, was the last game of Aguirre's college career. DePaul won 88 percent of its games in his three seasons.

"For me, college was about the learning experience, the education from Coach Meyer," Aguirre said. "At that point in my career was when I really learned how to play. It was exciting to go to practice and know every day you were going to find something out about the game."

**Height/Weight:** 6-6/230   **High School:** Westinghouse Vocational, Chicago   **College:** DePaul University, 1978-1981

# 52 Wayman TISDALE

## CAREER STATS

Career Pts: **2,661**

Scoring Avg: **25.6**

Rebounding Avg: **10.1**

Field Goal %: **.578**

### TOURNAMENT PLAY
**NCAA: 1983, 1984, 1985 (4-3)**

### AWARDS AND ACHIEVEMENTS
**Consensus
All-American, 1985**

**Consensus
All-American, 1984**

**Consensus
All-American, 1983**

*Born: June 9, 1964, Fort Worth, Texas*

## For Tisdale, it wasn't about tricking the defender into fouling. It was about overwhelming the opponent before he could consider how to react.

A rmed only with a lethal turnaround jumper and an infectious personality, Wayman Tisdale strolled into the center of Football Country and convinced the citizens of Oklahoma that basketball was worth loving, too.

Tisdale entered a program that reached the NCAA Tournament once in the previous 35 years. Not many Sooners fans really cared, so long as autumns were filled with football victories over Nebraska and Colorado.

Tisdale made basketball matter. Immediately. With 51 points in his fourth game, he broke the school record. He became MVP at the Rainbow Classic. By the close of the year, he was among the NCAA's top 10 scorers, the Sooners were a tournament team and he was the first freshman consensus All-American.

There wasn't the same cunning to Tisdale's low-post work evident in the style of Notre Dame's Adrian Dantley a decade earlier. For Tisdale, it wasn't about tricking the defender into fouling. It was about overwhelming the opponent before he could consider how to react. Tisdale got his massive frame airborne quickly after catching the ball near the lane. He scored 61 points in one game and fell short of double figures once in 104 games.

By his junior season, Oklahoma was a power. The Sooners advanced to the NCAA Sweet 16 as Tisdale averaged 28.5 points and 81 percent shooting. This set up a classic meeting against Louisiana Tech and big man Karl Malone. Tisdale scored 23 points and got 11 rebounds; Malone countered with 20 points and 16 rebounds. But Tisdale nailed a jump shot with six seconds left in overtime, and the Sooners advanced to the Midwest Region final with an 86-84 victory.

Tisdale had helped coach Billy Tubbs build a program that would reach the NCAA Tournament 17 times in 20 years and eventually visit two Final Fours. Had Tisdale remained for his senior year, he could have become the first four-time consensus All-American and challenged Pete Maravich for the NCAA's career scoring record, and he might have had the chance to play in the Final Four himself. Instead, Tisdale entered the NBA draft. A dozen years later, Oklahoma retired his No. 23 jersey. No football Sooner had been presented the same honor.

---

*Height/Weight: 6-8/240    High School: Washington High, Tulsa    College: University of Oklahoma, 1982-1985*

# 53 Akeem OLAJUWON

## CAREER STATS

**Career Pts: 1,332**

**Scoring Avg: 13.3**

**Rebounding Avg: 10.7**

**Field Goal %: .639**

## TOURNAMENT PLAY
**NCAA: 1982, 1983, 1984 (12-3)**

**NCAA Final Four: 1982, 1983, 1984**

## AWARDS AND ACHIEVEMENTS
**NCAA Tournament Most Outstanding Player, 1983**

**Consensus All-American, 1984**

*Born: Jan. 21, 1963, Lagos, Nigeria*

## (Olajuwon) was named Most Outstanding Player, one of 11 players in the tournament's 64-year history to win that award from a losing team.

He did not grow up dreaming of competing in the Final Four, of playing for North Carolina or UCLA, of achieving basketball greatness. He did not expect to live the American dream, to become "Akeem The Dream," to become the rush chairman of the Phi Slamma Jamma fraternity.

Akeem Olajuwon is college basketball's greatest import. He had the talent and drive to become a dominant player. Had that package been delivered in Dallas or San Antonio, his rise to prominence with the Houston Cougars would have been expected. Because he was born in Nigeria, the game might never have found him.

Olajuwon was a teenage soccer goalie and team handball star when his size and athleticism caught the attention of a local coach who introduced him to basketball. Olajuwon rapidly worked his way to Nigeria's national team. An American coaching in Africa suggested he consider attending a U.S. college. Upon visiting Houston, Olajuwon liked the warm weather and decided to stay.

His transition to American basketball was slow—at times, slower than he thought necessary. He redshirted as a freshman and was not a regular starter on the 1982 Final Four team. He was bothered by a lack of playing time and occasional public criticism from Houston coach Guy Lewis.

It took Olajuwon time to learn some tenets of post play, but his competitiveness, coordination and jumping ability made him a natural as a shot-blocker and rebounder. He was a more comfortable shooter than many his size who grew up in the U.S. playing the game daily.

Olajuwon became a force without regularly producing huge scoring numbers. He averaged only 13.9 points for the powerful team that lost to North Carolina State in the 1983 NCAA title game on Lorenzo Charles' buzzer-beating dunk. Olajuwon averaged 20.5 points, 20 rebounds and 9.5 blocks in the Final Four and was named Most Outstanding Player, one of 11 players in the tournament's 64-year history to win that award from a losing team.

In his final season, Olajuwon led the nation in field-goal percentage, rebounding and blocks. That season also ended with Houston falling in the NCAA title game, this time to Georgetown. Not every dream has a perfect ending, but this was close enough.

**Height/Weight:** 7-0/250     **High School:** Muslim Teachers College, Lagos     **College:** University of Houston, 1981-1984

# 54 Shane BATTIER

## CAREER STATS

Career Pts: **1,984**

Scoring Avg: **13.6**

Rebounding Avg: **6.1**

3-Point %: **.416**

## TOURNAMENT PLAY

NCAA: 1998, 1999, 2000, 2001 (16-3)

NCAA Final Four: 1999, 2001

NCAA Champion: 2001

## AWARDS AND ACHIEVEMENTS

Consensus All-American, 2001

NCAA Tournament Most Outstanding Player, 2001

NABC Defensive Player of the Year, 1999, 2000, 2001

*Born: Sept. 9, 1978, Birmingham, Mich.*

*"I came to Duke willing to do whatever it took to help win ballgames."*

— Shane Battier

For all the times he jumped into the path of a speeding opponent and—whether or not there was contact—fell hard to the floor, no circumstance better defined Shane Battier's hunger for victory than his basket with 3:33 remaining in the 2001 NCAA title game between Duke and Arizona.

With his Blue Devils ahead by three points, a teammate missed a shot and Battier frantically moved to prevent it from falling into the wrong hands. He raced from the right side of the lane, leaped and tapped the ball into the goal—with the back of his hand. Who had ever seen such a thing? Might we ever see such a thing again?

"I came to Duke willing to do whatever it took to help win ballgames," Battier said. And so he did. Never considered a dynamic athlete, he wrapped two stunning dunks around that amazing tip-in—three baskets in a two-minute period—and the Devils ended that game with a victory over Arizona that delivered their third NCAA championship. That was the 131st college victory for Battier, a figure matched only by Kentucky point guard Wayne Turner (1995-99).

Battier's gift for making long-range shots enabled Duke to spread its offense to open up driving lanes for teammates Jason Williams and Mike Dunleavy. Battier made 246 threes, accounting for more than a third of his points.

There are no NCAA statistics for charges taken, but Battier became notorious for his willingness to step in front of driving opponents to draw charges. This fearlessness helped him three times get elected the nation's defensive player of the year. Anyway, statistics do not capture the collective force of his contributions. Battier was as effective a leader as anyone has coached.

"He had a unique ability to make everybody around him better," said Mike Krzyzewski, his coach at Duke. "Usually, you think of that in a point guard. I had ultimate confidence in his decision-making. I think he came at a time when I could appreciate him the most. At a younger age, I might have tried to control him. That would have been a big mistake."

**Height/Weight: 6-8/220    High School: Detroit Country Day    College: Duke University, 1997-2001**

# 55 Alex GROZA

The 1949 NCAA championship game became a meeting of two of the game's great minds: Oklahoma A&M's Hank Iba and Kentucky's Adolph Rupp. As so many coaches insist, though, players win games. Iba had Bob Harris at center. Rupp had Alex Groza.

Iba believed Harris could defend Groza one-on-one. Rupp saw that matchup and, according to Wildcats guard Ralph Beard, issued this order: "Everything goes inside." The other four Kentucky starters scored a combined 16 points in that championship game, but Groza delivered 25 in Kentucky's 46-36 victory. His nine field goals matched the total for the entire A&M squad. Harris was disqualified with five fouls.

"Harris couldn't handle Groza," Beard said. "Alex was 6-7 and cat-quick. He could hook with either hand. He was a great passer. He was just a great player."

Groza's 1949 NCAA performance was one of the best in the tournament's history. In a first-round victory over Villanova, he scored 30 points. Given that the average team scored 54 points in that tournament, Groza's 27.3 average is even more remarkable. He became the only player to appear in at least two Final Fours and lead all scorers in every game he played.

Groza developed significantly as an offensive player in that senior season. He fell short of double figures only twice and produced five 30-point games, including 38 in a victory over Georgia. He scored 210 more points than as a junior—in five fewer games.

Although Groza had hoped to attend Ohio State, Kentucky showed greater interest. He played a handful of games in 1944-45 before being called to military service and spent the following year in the Army. He returned to rejoin the UK program in 1946-47, and the team compiled a 34-3 record but lost to Utah in the NIT championship. Beard called it "the worst time" for Kentucky.

In fact, the worst came in 1951, when Groza and Beard were among those implicated in point shaving that dated back to their UK days. That kept the pair out of the NBA and basketball's Hall of Fame. Given what they accomplished at Kentucky, it does not exclude them from a list of the college game's genuine greats.

## CAREER STATS

**Career Pts: 1,744**    **Scoring Avg: 14.5**
**TOURNAMENT PLAY:  NCAA: 1948, 1949 (6-0)**
**NCAA Final Four: 1948, 1949        NCAA Champion: 1948, 1949**
**NIT: 1947, 1949**
**AWARDS AND ACHIEVEMENTS:**
**NCAA Tournament Most Outstanding Player, 1949**
**NCAA Tournament Most Outstanding Player, 1948**
**Consensus All-American, 1949        Consensus All-American, 1947**

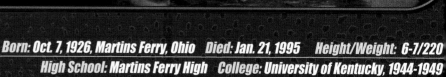

**Born: Oct. 7, 1926, Martins Ferry, Ohio    Died: Jan. 21, 1995    Height/Weight: 6-7/220**
**High School: Martins Ferry High    College: University of Kentucky, 1944-1949**

# Dan ISSEL 56

The finest scorer in Kentucky basketball did not have the same dream of becoming a Wildcat that led so many of the program's great players to Lexington. And Kentucky wasn't especially concerned about landing him.

Growing up near Chicago, Issel hoped to attend Wisconsin. UK coach Adolph Rupp wanted recruit George Janky to play center for him. "When I made my recruiting trip to Kentucky, I picked up the school newspaper and there was an article about the recruiting class," Issel said. "They named 15 people, and my name wasn't in it." When Janky instead chose Dayton, Issel was swayed by Rupp's redirected attention.

Issel discovered the Wildcats had signed 12 players to scholarships, and he was the last. He soon moved to the front of the pack. As a sophomore, Issel became the varsity's starting center. Most of the great players at that spot were 7-footers; Issel brought a different dimension by facing the basket and nailing 15-foot jump shots.

"Most centers played on the low post and had a few moves they could score on," Issel said. "Being able to shoot the 15-foot jump shot and put the ball on the floor, that was certainly a big asset."

Issel learned to play a different game from his prep coach, Don Vandersnick, who pushed him to develop his skills. Issel and his teammates would get to school 45 minutes early to work on shooting and free throws. After school, they'd practice three hours. Issel then would stay for additional instruction.

He progressed as a scorer each season at Kentucky, more than doubling his average from 16.4 his first season to 33.9 as a senior. He became a more confident and effective shooter and hit 55 percent in that last season. Though frustrated by two regional final losses that kept him from competing in the Final Four, he left UK with a treasured memory nonetheless.

Nine games from the close of the regular season, Kentucky visited Mississippi with Issel on the verge of setting the UK career scoring record. With his father in the audience, he sailed past Cotton Nash's standard with 53 points, also the school's best for a single game. Afterward, Rupp made a rare admission of fondness for one of his players. "I'm really glad you were able to achieve that record," he whispered to Issel, who was glad to have gotten the chance.

## CAREER STATS

**Career Pts: 2,138    Scoring Avg: 25.8**
**Rebounding Avg: 13.0    Field Goal %: .519**
**TOURNAMENT PLAY:   NCAA: 1968, 1969, 1970 (2-3)**
**AWARDS AND ACHIEVEMENTS: Consensus All-American, 1970**

*Born: Oct. 25, 1948, Batavia, Ill.    Height/Weight: 6-9/225*
*High School: Batavia High    College: University of Kentucky, 1967-1970*

# 57 James WORTHY

## CAREER STATS

**Career Pts: 1,219**

**Scoring Avg: 14.5**

**Rebounding Avg: 7.4**

**Field Goal %: .541**

**TOURNAMENT PLAY**
**NCAA: 1981, 1982 (9-1)**

**AWARDS AND ACHIEVEMENTS**
**NCAA Tournament Most Outstanding Player, 1982**

**Consensus All-American, 1982**

*Born: Feb. 27, 1961, Gastonia, N.C.*

## At 6-9, Worthy was as graceful as any forward, with long arms and quick feet that rendered of little consequence the fact he was not a dangerous jump shooter.

The greatest NCAA championship game ever televised is remembered for some of its indelible moments: Georgetown center Patrick Ewing goaltending five times in the first several minutes, the game-winning jumpshot by North Carolina guard Michael Jordan, the errant pass by Hoyas guard Fred Brown that secured the first national title for Tar Heels coach Dean Smith.

For all that transpired in those 40 minutes, nothing was of greater consequence than the play of Carolina forward James Worthy, who might have presented the best individual performance in seven decades of NCAA Tournament finals.

At 6-9, Worthy was as graceful as any forward, with long arms and quick feet that rendered of little consequence the fact he was not a dangerous jump shooter. He outran defenders when he had the room. In tighter quarters, he outquicked them. Smith admired Worthy's commitment to the total game, suggesting during the 1981-82 season that Worthy's defensive work "may be as good as any player we've had here."

Worthy was fortunate to be fully functioning again. He'd played the previous year with a metal rod and two screws binding his ankle because of a fracture that cost him half of his first Carolina season. He averaged 15.6 points as a junior, but attempted only 11 shots per game in a balanced attack. He could score more when necessary, as in his 26-point outburst against No. 2-rated Kentucky.

In the NCAA final, with Ewing threatening to block every shot, Worthy took command. He connected on 13-of-17 shots against the Hoyas. Many of those running dunks following turnovers or steals that diminished Ewing's ability to affect the game. Worthy scored 28 points. He also was the player who picked off that pass thrown by Brown, and it was less of an accident than it might have appeared.

"When I saw him pick up his dribble, I was like, 'Oh, boy, that was a no-no. He's panicking,'" Worthy later told THE SPORTING NEWS. "That's the worst thing you can do. I said, 'Here's my opportunity,' and I jumped out. I just knew he was going to throw it." Worthy did just about everything correctly that day—even forcing an opponent's mistake.

**Height/Weight:** *6-9/220*    **High School:** *Ashbrook High, Gastonia, N.C.*    **College:** *University of North Carolina, 1979-1982*

# 58 John WOODEN

hrough decades filled with more honors and flattery than any human could process, one compliment stuck with John Wooden about his time playing for Purdue. His coach, Ward "Piggy" Lambert, told Wooden he was the best-conditioned athlete and most unselfish player he had seen.

His 1960 Hall of Fame induction as a player might have been a bigger deal for Wooden, but not by a lot. He deeply respected Lambert and, as he reinforced during his years as UCLA coach, was deeply committed to the importance of fitness for an athlete. Wooden developed strong, thick legs and muscular arms from his hours of training. He rarely tired on the court.

"I really loved to play defense," Wooden said. "I liked to defend bigger men more often than men my own size, because I would be quicker."

He was a gifted ballhandler who developed a knack for the give-and-go. That remains a functional part of basketball offense, but then was an indispensable play. He developed another shot that required him to fake a step toward the basket, then spin the opposite direction and bank the ball off the board. "I worked hard on that," Wooden said. "I would say I scored more points on that than any other way."

Wooden shared much of the credit for his playing success with center Stretch Murphy, who stood 6-8 and dominated the center jumps that followed every basket under the rules of the day. The two were teammates in 1930 and both were named All-American. Wooden believed he might never have gained that level of recognition without the attention Murphy drew and the team success they achieved.

In their one year together, Purdue won 13 of its 15 games. During Wooden's three seasons, the composite record was 42-8. Wooden senior-year squad compiled a 17-1 mark and a Western Conference title and later gained recognition by the Helms Foundation as that year's national champion.

Wooden didn't rely entirely on quickness. He was unusually aggressive, throwing his body onto the court so often for loose balls that he picked up the nickname "Indiana Rubber Man." Through three seasons, he never lost the bounce in his step.

## CAREER STATS
**Career Pts: 475    Scoring Avg: 9.9**
**Assists: 7.7    Field Goal %: .468**
**AWARDS AND ACHIEVEMENTS:**
Helms Foundation College Player of the Year, 1932    Consensus All-American, 1932
Consensus All-American, 1931    Consensus All-American, 1930

Born: Oct. 14, 1910, Martinsville, Ind.   Height/Weight: 5-10/185   High School: Martinsville High   College: Purdue University, 1929-1932

# Gail GOODRICH 59

The dynasty began on March 20, 1965, and Gail Goodrich was largely the reason. To say he singlehandedly won the 1965 NCAA championship game would violate every principle coach John Wooden espoused at UCLA, but it was not far from true.

Goodrich scored 42 points in a 91-80 Bruins triumph over Michigan in Portland, Ore., making 18 of his 20 free-throw attempts. More than 1,200 players have appeared in the championship game, including Wilt Chamberlain, Kareem Abdul-Jabbar, Michael Jordan, and Larry Bird. Only one—Bill Walton, with 44 points in 1972—bettered that performance.

With that comfortable victory, UCLA claimed its second consecutive championship, and that commenced its decade-long reign over college basketball. That sort of dominance does not begin with a single title. As Wooden himself once said, "A lot of teams have won one in a row."

Goodrich was one of the first great lefthanders. He used his quickness to dart into defensive gaps and launch accurate jump shots from a variety of distances. Goodrich teamed with Walt Hazzard in one of the ultimate backcourts. Their pairing in 1964 led to a 30-0 season and NCAA title, the second unbeaten champion and one of seven overall, though the Bruins had no starter taller than 6-5.

Goodrich had grown from a 135-pound freshman who picked up the nickname "Twig" into a scoring genius by the time he arrived in the NCAA Tournament his senior year. He averaged 35 points in the four victories necessary to claim the title, the seventh-best average in the event's history. It was an even more astonishing achievement given Wooden's constant emphasis on the value of team play.

"From an offensive standpoint, Coach Wooden taught everyone at UCLA about teamwork, about balance," Goodrich said. "Like most really good high school players, I was the sort of player who needed the ball. What I learned at UCLA was to play without the ball. Coach told me there were 40 minutes in the game, the offense had the ball for 20, and if you divide that by five, that's four minutes when you have the ball in your hand. You've got to do something the other 36 minutes."

## CAREER STATS

**Career Pts: 1,690    Scoring Avg: 19.0    Rebounding Avg: 4.7**
**Field Goal %: .476    TOURNAMENT PLAY:    NCAA: 1963, 1964, 1965, (8-1)**
**NCAA Final Four: 1964, 1965    NCAA Champion: 1964, 1965**
**AWARDS AND ACHIEVEMENTS:**
**Consensus All-American, 1965**

**Born: April 23, 1943, Los Angeles    Height/Weight: 6-1/175    High School: Los Angeles Polytechnic    College: UCLA, 1962-1965**

# 60 Wes UNSELD

As a center in the NBA, Wes Unseld had to contend with an obvious height disadvantage against 7-footers such as Wilt Chamberlain and Kareem Abdul-Jabbar. It was only a little different from what he became used to during his days at Louisville. "I was small even in college," Unseld said. "But because of college, because of Peck Hickman, I was coached how to do it. It didn't matter if I was short or not."

Heckman was Unseld's first coach at Louisville, and Unseld credits him with teaching the fundamentals necessary for someone his size to survive in a land of giants. Unseld was a giant, too, but only if measured in terms of width. His bulk and strength helped him seize the necessary space to function against taller players, but the instinct he polished and the intelligence he developed led him to excel.

He established Louisville's single-game scoring record with 45 points against Georgetown College and still holds career records for scoring and rebounding averages. He produced eight of Louisville's top-10 rebounding performances. There are few big men, if any, who became as respected as Unseld based on rebounding and passing. "But I could score, too," he said.

Unseld teamed with gifted young guard Butch Beard to lead the Cardinals to a 23-5 record in the 1966-67 season. They ended with the No. 2 ranking in the final wire-service polls, but dropped a first-round NCAA Tournament game to SMU despite Unseld's 18 points and 12 rebounds.

Like all players of his era, Unseld was not permitted to compete as a freshman. He averaged 35.8 points and 23.6 rebounds with the Louisville freshman team. Those stats did not go on his permanent record, but an exhibition game against the Cardinals varsity that year—a team that went on to play in the NIT—created an indelible memory.

"We killed them," Unseld said. "If there was a game that stood out, that was it for me. It let me know that maybe I could play big-time college basketball." Unseld knew he could be a center for the Cardinals. He knew he could be whatever he wanted to be.

*Born: March 14, 1946, Louisville, Ky.*

*"I was small even in college. But because of college, because of Peck Hickman, I was coached how to do it. It didn't matter if I was short or not."*

— Wes Unseld

## CAREER STATS

Career Pts: **1,686**

Scoring Avg: **20.6**

Rebounding Avg: **18.9**

Field Goal %: **.558**

**TOURNAMENT PLAY**
NCAA: 1967, 1968
(0-2)

**AWARDS AND ACHIEVEMENTS**
Consensus
All-American, 1968

Consensus
All-American, 1967

*Height/Weight:* **6-7/230**   *High School:* **Seneca High, Louisville**   *College:* **University of Louisville, 1965-1968**

# 61 Lennie ROSENBLUTH

## CAREER STATS

**Career Pts:** 2,045

**Scoring Avg:** 26.9

**Rebounding Avg:** 10.4

**Field Goal %:** .459

### TOURNAMENT PLAY
**NCAA: 1957 (5-0)**

**NCAA Final Four: 1957**

**NCAA Champion: 1957**

### AWARDS AND ACHIEVEMENTS
**Helms Foundation Player of the Year, 1957**

**Consensus All-American, 1957**

*Born: Jan. 22, 1933, New York*

## Rosenbluth had a city player's slick moves and gift for the unexpected. He was unafraid to shoot in traffic, or off balance, or falling away from the goal. ...

It seemed impossible anyone other than Wilt Chamberlain would become the preeminent figure of the 1956-57 season. The basketball world had waited eagerly for the Kansas debut of this 7-1 giant. It was almost certain he would be the greatest player on the best team. He instead was usurped by North Carolina's Lennie Rosenbluth, who led the Tar Heels to perfection.

With Rosenbluth averaging 28 points and shooting 48 percent from the field, North Carolina won all 32 of its games. The Tar Heels were a cohesive unit of mostly New York natives conscripted by UNC's coach, Greenwich Village product Frank McGuire. They operated seamlessly as a team, and one thing they agreed upon was Rosenbluth should attempt most of the shots.

He was North Carolina's top scorer in 27 of those 32 victories. Rosenbluth had a city player's slick moves and gift for the unexpected. He was unafraid to shoot in traffic, or off balance, or falling away from the goal. He performed well under pressure, nailing a hook for a game-winning basket against Wake Forest in the ACC Tournament and averaging 37.5 points in two games against rival Duke. He became the ACC's player of the year and tournament MVP.

His importance to the Tar Heels never was more apparent than in the national semifinals against Michigan State. Though it was not his most efficient performance, Rosenbluth took 42 shots to produce 29 points that led the Tar Heels. They needed three overtimes to win, but the victory put them in position to face Kansas in the championship game. Rosenbluth fouled out against KU after scoring 20 of North Carolina's 46 regulation-time points. UNC again had to enter triple overtime, but it beat Kansas without him.

For all of that, Rosenbluth never was entirely comfortable as the object of attention. He did what was expected, what was necessary, but did not demand to be the offensive focus.

It is notable that his record 26.9-point career scoring average held up through perhaps the greatest individual talent parade any program has enjoyed: Bob McAdoo, Phil Ford, James Worthy, Michael Jordan, Antawn Jamison. None of those players bettered that mark. None of them approached it. And none played on a perfect team.

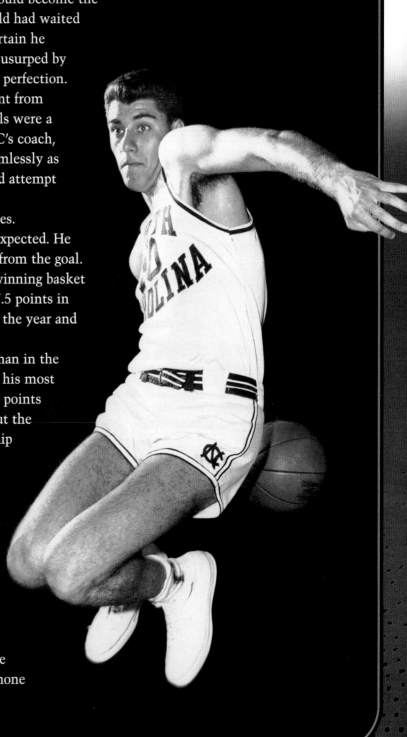

*Height/Weight: 6-5/180   High School: Monroe High, Bronx, N.Y.   College: University of North Carolina, 1954-1957*

# 62 Glenn ROBINSON

In more than two decades as Purdue coach, Gene Keady earned six Big Ten championships with few great individual talents. When Keady finally landed a star, it was one of the brightest.

Power forward Glenn Robinson grew up a little more than an hour from the Purdue campus, in the industrial city of Gary. As an eighth-grader, he attended Keady's summer camp. The coach immediately recognized a likely future star. After Robinson became a Boilermaker, he helped the program achieve one of its finest seasons with one of the greatest performances ever by a college player.

Robinson dominated 1993-94 as no player had controlled college basketball in nearly 20 years. He had size and quickness and natural scoring moves to collect baskets in the post. He was proficient enough as a 3-point shooter to connect on 38 percent of his attempts. In an era when few players were comfortable attempting shots between those two extremes, the springy Robinson could launch from the foul line after a quick dribble to clear himself or fire a 12-foot turnaround jumper after catching a teammate's pass.

He saved his most brilliant performance for the final victory of his Purdue career, scoring 44 points against Kansas in the NCAA Tournament's round of 16, a game Purdue won by five. The biggest moment in his biggest game occurred when Robinson soared over 7-2 center Greg Ostertag for a two-handed slam dunk.

Admiring Robinson's unselfishness, Keady said, "He didn't shoot unexpected shots." That was only true for his teammates. Opponents never became comfortable defending someone so resourceful. In four games against Big Ten powers Michigan and Indiana that season, Robinson averaged 36.3 points.

"He had a great sense of what was a good shot," Keady said. Robinson fit into the Purdue program because he made no demands for star treatment. In his final season, the Boilers finished 29-5, losing in the Southeast Region final to Duke.

"He wasn't playing for Glenn. He played for the team," Keady said. "In his first year, we were playing at Southwest Missouri State and won by two when Herb Dove got a steal late in the game to end it. Glenn scored two points in that game, and it was probably the happiest I've ever seen him."

*Born: Jan. 10, 1973, Gary, Ind.*

**"He wasn't playing for Glenn. He played for the team."**

—Gene Keady

## CAREER STATS

Career Pts: **1,706**

Scoring Avg: **27.5**

Rebounding Avg: **9.7**

Field Goal %: **.479**

### TOURNAMENT PLAY
NCAA: 1993, 1994
(3-2)

### AWARDS AND ACHIEVEMENTS
Robertson Trophy,
Naismith Award,
Wooden Award, 1994

Consensus
All-American, 1994

*Height/Weight: 6-7/220    High School: Roosevelt High, Gary    College: Purdue University, 1992-1994*

# 63 Marques JOHNSON

## CAREER STATS

**Career Pts:** 1,659 **Scoring Avg:** 14.4 **Assists:** 7.8 **Field Goal %:** .568

**TOURNAMENT PLAY:** NCAA: 1974, 1975, 1976, 1977 (11-3) **NCAA Final Four:** 1974, 1975, 1976 **NCAA Champion:** 1975

**AWARDS AND ACHIEVEMENTS:** Wooden Award, Naismith Award, Robertson Trophy, 1977 Consensus All-American, 1977

*Born: Feb. 8, 1956, Los Angeles*

## "This is my destiny. I need to go out there and be a dunking fool."

—Marques Johnson

He grew up in Los Angeles certain he would attend UCLA, play four years for the great John Wooden and become an essential part of extending the Bruins' string of NCAA championships on toward infinity. Not everything worked out as Marques Johnson envisioned it, but his career played out like a dream.

Johnson played for the Bruins. "Once UCLA came calling my junior year in high school," Johnson says, "it was pretty much a done deal." Wooden coached him as a freshman and sophomore, but his retirement in 1975 led to Gene Bartow taking over the program.

There was only one championship in Johnson's four seasons. The Bruins lost in the national semifinals in 1974 and 1976. In Johnson's senior year, they fell short of the Final Four for the first time in a decade.

However, Johnson was a huge reason Wooden ended his career with the glory of a title-game triumph over Kentucky. In the West Region final against Arizona State, Johnson contributed 35 points and 12 rebounds and that led to a 14-point Bruins victory.

Johnson had contracted hepatitis just as preseason practice was to begin in October 1974. He averaged 11.6 points in a year he expected to "just dominate." Against Arizona State, his legs felt fresh and his jump shot began falling. The game was in Portland, where former Bruins star Sidney Wicks played professionally. "He came down at halftime and was yelling at me to keep taking it to the hole, keep shooting the jumper," Johnson said. "He was my boyhood idol, my favorite player. I had the game of my life."

Although there was no championship in his final season and no John Wooden to coach him, Johnson did claim the first John R. Wooden Award, presented in 1977 and every year since to the nation's top collegian.

"That was the first year they put the dunk back in, and it was like, 'This is my destiny. I need to go out there and be a dunking fool,' " Johnson said. "I'd set my sights on winning the Wooden Award, and I wanted to electrify the voters. It was another case of the stars lining up for me."

*Height/Weight:* **6-7/225**   *High School:* **Crenshaw High, Los Angeles**   *College:* **UCLA, 1973-1977**

# 64 Paul ARIZIN

Some athletes are celebrated for what they accomplish, some for how they accomplish it. Paul Arizin fits both categories. Spreading the popularity of the jump shot placed him among the game's innovators, but Arizin also ranks as one of the finest scoring forwards.

Arizin's role in the development of the jump shot was similar to Henry Ford's work with the automobile. Ford didn't invent the car, but he transformed it from a luxury to a common possession.

There might have been other jump shooters before Arizin, but he made it fashionable by leading the nation in scoring in 1950 with 25.3 points per game and with his school-record 85-point performance against the Naval Air Materiel Center in February 1949. In that game, he scored 23 points in the first seven minutes following halftime. He took all but two of the team's shots in the second half.

The jump shot was in the early stages of its evolution when Arizin brought it to a wider stage. His technique has been compared to that of a shot-putter. Arizin was adept at driving the ball, and his jumping ability made him effective around the boards. He later estimated only a fraction of his points were scored on jumpers—but then, only a small portion of Julius Erving's and David Thompson's points came from dunks. The sensational is what is remembered.

At LaSalle High in Philadelphia, Arizin played a few games before being cut. He admitted he wasn't good enough to play on a team that won a city championship. After enrolling at Villanova as a chemistry major, he improved by playing in his free time. He competed in a tournament in the campus gym, and his team wound up in the championship game opposite the Villanova varsity. After Arizin was named MVP, he began fielding scholarship offers from other Philadelphia colleges. Wildcats coach Alex Severance chose not to let him get away.

Arizin became Villanova's first 1,000-point scorer and helped lead the team to the 1949 NCAA Tournament by averaging 22 points per game. Villanova had a solid team but lacked outstanding shooters. Arizin's jump shot immediately made him the primary scoring option. It made him one of basketball's most important figures, as well.

**Career Pts: 1,596   Scoring Avg: 20.0**
**TOURNAMENT PLAY: NCAA: 1949 (0-1)**
**AWARDS AND ACHIEVEMENTS: The Sporting News Player of the Year, 1950**
**Consensus All-American, 1950**

*Born: April 9, 1928, Philadelphia   Height/Weight: 6-3/185   High School: La Salle High, Philadelphia   College: Villanova University, 1947-1950*

# Artis GILMORE 65

Jacksonville University ranked as one of the smallest schools to reach the NCAA Final Four. Artis Gilmore became one of the largest players to succeed on that stage.

Gilmore stood 7-2, the same height as UCLA's Lew Alcindor, but Gilmore brought more muscle and power to the floor. He lifted Jacksonville toward the top of the basketball world for a fling that included a trip to the 1970 NCAA championship game.

The university had only 3,000 students and was in its 13th season competing as a four-year school. Gilmore was recruited almost by accident, when coach Joe Williams went after Gardner-Webb's Ernie Fleming and Fleming mentioned that the team had a 7-foot center. During Gilmore's recruitment, when Williams allowed the Jacksonville program did not have a national reputation, Gilmore's response was telling: "Don't worry, we'll get one."

In both his seasons at JU, Gilmore led the nation in rebounding. He became one of six players to finish with career averages of 20 or better in points and rebounds. He is the NCAA's career leader in rebounding average.

Although Gilmore compiled breathtaking averages of 26.5 points and 22.2 rebounds during the 1969-70 regular season, which Jacksonville concluded at 23-1, he was not a first-team All-American. Voters did not take his team and its competition seriously. In the NCAA Tournament, though, Gilmore conjured 30-point performances against Western Kentucky, which featured 7-footer Jim McDaniels, and Iowa, which had gone unbeaten in the Big Ten. He scored 24 points and got 20 rebounds in the regional final victory over Kentucky, which had been ranked No. 1.

Gilmore's poorest game came in the final. He had 19 points and 16 rebounds. The Dolphins lost by 11 to UCLA. Bruins coach John Wooden feared Gilmore's influence enough to double-team him with All-American Sidney Wicks playing behind him and 6-9 center Steve Patterson stationed in front.

Playing basketball at Gilmore's size did have its drawbacks. Some expected him to be Alcindor's equal merely because he was of equal size. They were different players, though, and chose different paths. Alcindor won three consecutive NCAA titles at UCLA. Gilmore got Jacksonville to the title game. Given the circumstances, that might have been a bigger deal.

## CAREER STATS

Career Pts: **1,312**   Scoring Avg: **24.3**
Rebounding Avg: **22.7**   Field Goal %: **.574**
TOURNAMENT PLAY:   NCAA: 1970, 1971 (4-2)   NCAA Final Four: 1970
AWARDS AND ACHIEVEMENTS: Consensus All-American, 1971

Born: *Sept. 21, 1949, Chipley, Fla.*   Height/Weight: *7-2/250*   High School: *Carver High, Dothan Ala.*
College: *Gardner-Webb Junior College—Jacksonville University, 1969-1971*

# 66 Shaquille O'NEAL

## CAREER STATS

**Career Pts:** 1,941

**Scoring Avg:** 21.6

**Rebounding Avg:** 13.5

**Field Goal %:** .610

## TOURNAMENT PLAY
**NCAA: 1990, 1991, 1992 (2-3)**

## AWARDS AND ACHIEVEMENTS
**Associated Press Player of the Year, 1991**

**Consensus All-American, 1992**

**Consensus All-American, 1991**

*Born: March 6, 1972, Newark, N.J.*

# "I was telling someone we were going to play a box-and-one defense against him. But I think we would have had a problem with our one guy trying to guard LSU's four other guys."

## —Ed Murphy

Of all the astonishing things Shaquille O'Neal did during three seasons of basketball at LSU, perhaps the most astonishing is simply that he played three seasons.

O'Neal was so physically imposing he could have been the No. 1 overall pick following either of his first two years with the Tigers. But even after claiming one national player of the year award as a sophomore, O'Neal stuck around and insisted there was much he needed to learn about basketball. As the sport moved toward amateur players devaluing their education in the game and rushing to the NBA as rapidly as possible, O'Neal was almost a dinosaur.

He was big enough. O'Neal stood 7-1, 290 pounds and packed agility, ferocity and leaping ability into that package. Coaches who opposed him had no idea how to deal with him and expressed their respect in postgame quotes:

"The thing we wanted to do was have three guys around him," said Arizona's Lute Olson after a 10-point defeat. "And he still got the shots off."

"I was telling someone we were going to play a box-and-one defense against him," said Ed Murphy, coach at Mississippi. "But I think we would have had a problem with our one guy trying to guard LSU's four other guys."

After the Tigers defeated Kentucky behind O'Neal's 20 points, 20 rebounds and six blocks, Wildcats coach Rick Pitino called it "an average game." The ultimate compliment, perhaps.

Given the breadth of his talents, much of what is remembered about O'Neal's career is what he and his teams did not do. Three NCAA Tournament appearances ended short of the Sweet 16. As if it were his fault.

In his junior season, LSU's backcourt struggled and the Tigers entered the tournament with a 20-9 record, good for only a No. 7 seed. That meant a second-round matchup with Indiana, which earned an 89-79 victory but not before O'Neal scored 36 points, including 27 of his team's 41 second-half points. He also had 12 rebounds and five blocked shots.

O'Neal walked off the court in Boise, Idaho, with a tear in his eye and got a gentle peck on the cheek from LSU coach Dale Brown. They were kissing an era goodbye.

**Height/Weight: 7-1/290    High School: Cole High, San Antonio    College: Louisiana State University, 1989-1992**

# 67 Adrian DANTLEY

## CAREER STATS

**Career Pts: 2,223**

**Scoring Avg: 25.8**

**Rebounding Avg: 9.8**

**Field Goal %: .562**

## TOURNAMENT PLAY
**NCAA: 1974, 1975, 1976 (3-3)**

## AWARDS AND ACHIEVEMENTS
**Robertson Trophy, 1976**

**Consensus All-American, 1976**

**Consensus All-American, 1975**

*Born: Feb. 28, 1956, Washington, D.C.*

> ## "You hear a lot of players say, 'Yeah, I want the ball.' But I prided myself on taking good shots."
>
> —Adrian Dantley

When he arrived at Notre Dame packing a few extra pounds of padding, Adrian Dantley picked up a tag that was slow to fade as he continued his career: "chubby." He never liked it, though it never prevented him from starring with the Fighting Irish.

He weighed 230 pounds in his freshman season, when he started for one of the top teams in the nation, the team that ended UCLA's record winning streak. Dantley prefers to remember himself as "thick" at that stage of his career. "I wasn't fat, and I don't know where they got 'chubby.' " But in the NCAA Tournament loss to Michigan that ended that team's season at 26-3, Dantley struggled to shake the Wolverines' Wayman Britt and became determined to play in better physical condition.

As a sophomore and junior, he weighed closer to 220 pounds and became nearly unstoppable as an inside scoring force. He used his still-ample behind to uproot defenders while positioning in the low post and was so clever drawing fouls he earned more points at the free-throw line than seven of the NCAA's top 10 career scorers. Dantley averaged 30.4 points his second year and ranked No. 2 in Division I. In his junior year, Dantley attempted three fewer shots per game and scored 28.6 points, the nation's fourth-ranked output. He accounted for the vast majority of Notre Dame's offense in those last two seasons, carrying an extraordinary offensive burden.

"There aren't that many players that can handle that responsibility," Dantley said. "You hear a lot of players say, 'Yeah, I want the ball.' But I prided myself on taking good shots."

On the most important play of his career, Dantley wasn't asked to shoot. On January 19, 1974, at Notre Dame's Athletic and Convocation Center, the Irish were down a point in the final 10 seconds and got the ball to guard Dwight Clay in the right corner. He cut loose a floating jumper that snapped through the net and gave Notre Dame a 71-70 win over UCLA, ending the Bruins' 88-game victory streak.

"I was right under the basket," Dantley said, "ready to get the offensive rebound in case he missed. That was the biggest highlight of my career."

**Height/Weight:** 6-5/220   **High School:** DeMatha Catholic, Hyattsville, Md.   **College:** Notre Dame University, 1973-1976

# 68 Sean ELLIOTT

## CAREER STATS

**Career Pts: 2,555**

**Scoring Avg: 19.2**

**Rebounding Avg: 6.1**

**Field Goal %: .512**

**TOURNAMENT PLAY**
NCAA: 1986, 1987, 1988, 1989 (6-4)

**NCAA Final Four: 1988**

**AWARDS AND ACHIEVEMENTS**
Wooden Award, 1989

Consensus
All-American, 1989

Consensus
All-American, 1988

*Born: Feb. 2, 1968, Tucson, Ariz.*

> ## *"Absolutely no one can stop Sean one-on-one. Offensively, there isn't anything that Sean can't do."*
>
> —Lute Olson

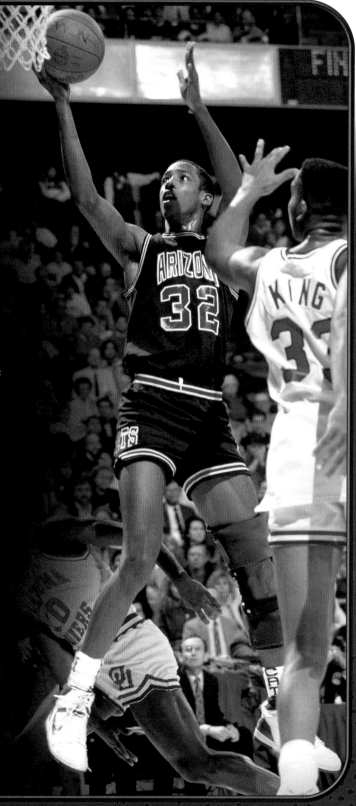

ean Elliott and Arizona basketball came of age at the same moment in the most unlikely place: on a snowy winter weekend in Anchorage, Alaska, a weekend when the Earth shook and the basketball landscape was fundamentally altered.

The 1987 Great Alaska Shootout ranked with the best in-season tournaments ever contested. Syracuse was coming off its NCAA title-game appearance the previous March and featured stars Derrick Coleman and Sherman Douglas. The majority of Michigan's players returned the following season and claimed the 1989 NCAA title. In this company, the team that stood out was Arizona, and Elliott stood above everyone.

The Wildcats had made NCAA Tournament appearances in each of the previous two years but were eliminated in the opening round. Elliott was one of the Pacific-10's best players, but the lack of tournament success limited his national recognition.

On the morning of the championship game matching Arizona and Syracuse, an earthquake off the southern coast gave Anchorage a slight shake. There was no damage in the city, but Syracuse later tumbled under the weight of Elliott's varied skills: his speed in driving the ball, his sweet shooting touch, his vision as a passer. Arizona's Shootout victories over Duquesne, Michigan and Syracuse were by an average of 27 points. Four months later, the Wildcats were in the 1988 Final Four.

"Absolutely no one can stop Sean one-on-one," Olson told the Kansas City Star before the Wildcats competed at Kemper Arena. "Offensively, there isn't anything that Sean can't do."

Elliott became Olson's most important Arizona recruit. It wasn't a matter of winning an extended battle for a coveted prospect and gaining credibility. Elliott was not widely recruited until late in his career. This was about landing someone who could push the team forward on the floor.

For the Final Four team, Elliott shot 57 percent from the floor, 47 percent on 3-pointers and averaged 19.2 points. His height allowed him to see over defenders and into the lane and led to 3.6 assists per game. In his final two years, the Wildcats were 64-7 and twice earned No. 1 NCAA seeds. Elliott had turned Arizona into one of the nation's hottest programs.

**Height/Weight:** *6-8/210*  **High School:** *Cholla High, Tucson*  **College:** *University of Arizona, 1985-1989*

# 69 Antawn JAMISON

He wasn't much of a jump shooter. He didn't have the bulk to bang with the big guys. He couldn't handle the ball well enough to drive it from the wings. So how could it be that Antawn Jamison averaged just short of 20 points for his North Carolina career?

Jamison overcame his limitations by inventing his own unique style. If he couldn't shoot from long distances, his attempts would come from in close. If he couldn't jostle with powerful players, he would move too fast for them to catch him. If he couldn't handle the ball, he'd transact his business quickly.

In a spectacular game against Duke in February 1998, Jamison scored 35 points by making 14 of his 20 shots from the field. Somebody put a stopwatch on his performance that night and discovered the ball touched his hands for only 53 seconds.

His signature shot was a jump-hook launched from a release point so high few could reach to block it and cut loose so quickly it always was too late to try. Steve Robinson, who coached Florida State against North Carolina, said Jamison "knows where he's going with the ball even before it gets to his hand."

Jamison was a great offensive rebounder when he entered the Carolina program, which led to many of his points. Coach Dean Smith gradually taught him how to use his body to establish offensive position. Jamison was willing to set up for that jump-hook even if he was 14 feet from the basket. To gain confidence, he practiced it from the 3-point line.

The star player for two North Carolina teams that reached the NCAA Final Four, Jamison fell short of delivering Tar Heels fans their fourth national championship. They had to settle for something nearly as rewarding: Jamison playing his best against Duke, the Heels' fiercest rival.

In three home games against the Blue Devils, Jamison averaged 30.3 points and 12.0 rebounds. Most important, North Carolina won five of seven meetings, including the 1998 ACC Tournament championship. "To beat someone like that," said Duke coach Mike Krzyzewski, "you hope they let down." He understood that surely was not Jamison's style.

*Born: June 12, 1976, Shreveport, La.*

**"(Jamison) knows where he's going with the ball even before it gets to his hand."**

— Steve Robinson

## CAREER STATS

Career Pts: **1,974**

Scoring Avg: **19.0**

Rebounding Avg: **9.9**

Field Goal %: **.577**

### TOURNAMENT PLAY
**NCAA: 1996, 1997, 1998 (9-3)**

**NCAA Final Four: 1997, 1998**

### AWARDS AND ACHIEVEMENTS
**Robertson Trophy, Naismith Award, Wooden Award, 1998**

**Consensus All-American, 1998**

*Height/Weight: 6-9/220   High School: Providence High, Charlotte   College: University of North Carolina, 1995-1998*

# 70 Len BIAS

If only Len Bias' career at Maryland had not ended so soon. The Terps played two games in the NCAA Tournament during his senior year, losing the second to UNLV by a mere six points. If only there had been more of him to remember.

With each game, his influence swelled. His performance in the 1986 ACC Tournament enabled a Maryland squad that struggled during the regular season to score a huge upset over No. 4 North Carolina. Attacking as though he might never play again, Bias scored 20 points and grabbed 13 rebounds. Behind Bias' 20 points and seven rebounds, the Terps lost by just two points to No. 6 Georgia Tech in the semifinals. Had Maryland not achieved that league tournament success, Bias might have been forced to finish his glorious career in the NIT.

In his final competitive game, Bias contributed 31 of his team's 64 points and grabbed 12 rebounds. When he finished, Bias had created a career that ranked with the most appealing success stories of the 1980s. He averaged only 7.2 points as a freshman, struggling to crack a veteran lineup. He had not yet matured physically and still was expanding the range on his jump shot.

With each year at Maryland, he dramatically improved—all the way to the 23.2 scoring average that led the ACC his senior year. He was at his best in important games and averaged 18.7 points in nine NCAA Tournament games. Bias worked the baseline and used his muscle, jumping ability and smooth, reliable shooting form. Bias was one of those rare athletes capable not only of elevating a team, but carrying it. He was popular among teammates, who considered him generous with the basketball and with praise.

Three months after his last Maryland game, Bias was selected by the Boston Celtics with the No. 2 pick in the NBA draft. He celebrated with some friends and inhaled cocaine that apparently sent him into cardiac arrest. He died at age 22.

Bias became slightly larger in death. In the immediate aftermath, his coach at Maryland, Lefty Driesell, called Bias "the greatest basketball player that ever played in the Atlantic Coast Conference."

It was enough that he was close.

**Born: Nov. 18, 1963, Landover, Md.   Died: June 19, 1986**

# "...The greatest basketball player that ever played in the Atlantic Coast Conference."

—Lefty Driesell

## CAREER STATS

Career Pts: **2,149**

Scoring Avg: **16.4**

Rebounding Avg: **5.7**

Field Goal %: **.536**

**TOURNAMENT PLAY**
NCAA: 1983, 1984, 1985, 1986 (5-4)

**AWARDS AND ACHIEVEMENTS**
Consensus All-American, 1986

*Height/Weight: 6-8/220    High School: Northwestern High, Adelphi, Md.    College: University of Maryland, 1982-1986*

# 71 Danny FERRY

There was a simple reason Danny Ferry was called upon to occasionally ferry the ball upcourt for Duke: he could do it, and most of the other Blue Devils could not. That he stood 6-10 and played mostly at center was not an issue.

When Devils point guard Quin Snyder found himself in trouble, Ferry was the player expected to rescue him. There were no other comfortable ballhandlers in the rotation. "He got the chance, some of it from necessity," said Mike Krzyzewski, his coach at Duke. "And when he was doing it, I thought, 'Hey, this is kind of unique.' "

Ferry had a big man's body, with wide shoulders that facilitated battling along the baseline, but what separated him from others was his exquisite skill in handling, shooting and passing. His 506 career assists rank him fifth on Duke's career list, and he is the only big man among the top 10. He made just under 39 percent of his 3-point attempts. His ventures into advancing the ball helped the Devils advance to the NCAA Final Four in his final two seasons, thought they weren't favored to make it either time.

"He could shoot it, drive it, hit free throws," Krzyzewski said. "You just wanted the ball in his hands. He had a great understanding of the game."

For all the many tasks he could handle as a player, he was not one to hide behind his versatility. He was willing to assume the responsibility of taking over games. He set an Atlantic Coast Conference scoring record with 58 points in a game against Miami, making 23 of his 26 shots. He led the league in scoring as a senior, with a 22.6 average. In the final game of his career, at the Final Four in Seattle's Kingdome, he delivered 34 points that represented nearly half of Duke's total but weren't enough to prevent Seton Hall from advancing to the championship game.

"We made the Final Four a couple times when we probably shouldn't have because he was so good," Krzyzewski said. "Some people might say, 'You didn't win it,' but we wouldn't have made it unless this guy put us on his back."

*Born: Oct. 17, 1966, Hyattsville, Md.*

*"He could shoot it, drive it, hit free throws. You just wanted the ball in his hands. He had a great understanding of the game."*

—Mike Krzyzewski

### CAREER STATS

Career Pts: **2,155**

Scoring Avg: **15.1**

Rebounds Avg: **7.0**

Assists Avg: **3.5**

### TOURNAMENT PLAY
**NCAA: 1986, 1987, 1988, 1989 (15-4)**

**NCAA Final Four: 1986, 1988, 1989**

### AWARDS AND ACHIEVEMENTS
**Oscar Robertson Trophy, Naismith Award, 1989**

**Consensus All-American, 1989**

**The Sporting News All-American, 1988**

*Height/Weight:* **6-10/230**　　*High School:* **DeMatha Catholic, Hyattsville**　　*College:* **Duke University, 1985-1989**

# 72 Keith LEE

It seems impossible to discuss Keith Lee's career without starting with his hands. "He could absolutely catch, shoot and pass it as well as anybody that's ever played in college basketball," said Dana Kirk, Lee's coach at Memphis State. His hands were at the end of arms that resembled the wings of a condor, and they hungrily snatched up the basketball whenever it was nearby.

Lee's ability to run and jump was compromised by chronic knee problems. Memphis State occasionally had to slow its attack until he changed ends of the floor, but he was worth the wait. In an era teeming with athletic big men whose games flourished above the rim, Lee employed a ground-based attack that kept him on the same high plane as Georgetown's Patrick Ewing and Houston's Akeem Olajuwon.

Because of his skill with the ball and the low-post abilities of teammates William Bedford and Vincent Askew—and because it routinely required him to cover less of the court—Lee often was positioned in the high post. He was encouraged to strike with foul-line jump shots or draw the defense away from the goal and pass the ball inside. "He could pass as well as a point guard," Kirk said.

Lee's appearance in the 1985 Final Four amounted to a frustrating 23-minute cameo against Villanova in which he sat long stretches because of foul trouble and was disqualified after scoring 10 points. His finest moment did come in the NCAA Tournament, though, in a 1983 matchup against Ewing. Both were sophomores, but playing in the high-profile Big East had allowed Ewing to develop the greater reputation. In that second-round tournament game, Lee finished a 66-57 Memphis State victory with 28 points and 15 rebounds, compared to Ewing's 24 and nine. The Tigers won easily and became the only team to knock Georgetown out of the tournament short of the Final Four during Ewing's four-year career.

"If you had to draw up the way you wanted a big man to play a ballgame, that was the one right there," Kirk said. "Ewing kept looking over to John Thompson with frustration on his face. He could not guard Keith 15 feet from the basket."

*Born: Dec. 28, 1962, West Memphis, Ark.*

*He could absolutely catch, shoot and pass it as well as anybody that's ever played in college basketball."*

—Dana Kirk

## CAREER STATS

**Career Pts: 2,408**

**Scoring Avg: 18.8**

**Rebounds Avg: 10.4**

**Blocked Shots Avg: 2.5**

**TOURNAMENT PLAY**
NCAA: 1982, 1983, 1984, 1985 (8-4)

NCAA Final Four: 1985

**AWARDS AND ACHIEVEMENTS**
Consensus All-American, 1985

Consensus All-American, 1983

*Height/Weight:* **6-10/220**  *High School:* **West Memphis High**  *College:* **Memphis State University, 1981-1985**

# 73 Jim McDANIELS

The dunk was banned from NCAA basketball in 1967, the year Jim McDaniels arrived on Western Kentucky's campus. It remained a felony for the whole of his college career. Though he was a 7-0 center, it did not matter to him in the least. McDaniels was a shooter, not a slammer.

McDaniels was as comfortable squeezing off a 14-foot jumper as standing beneath the basket and banking in a layup. The face-up jumper that made McDaniels an offensive force was developed as a teenager, when he was so much taller than the kids he faced on playgrounds that they surrounded the basket and refused to let him approach. He began shooting from beyond that boundary and developed a touch that made him the leading scorer among big men in 1970-71.

As a senior, McDaniels ranked No. 5 among major-college scorers at 29.3 points per game, and Western Kentucky improbably reached the Final Four with tournament victories over Jacksonville, Kentucky and Ohio State.

Twice that year, McDaniels faced fellow 7-footer Artis Gilmore of Jacksonville. The first was played at Louisville's Freedom Hall, and McDaniels besieged the Dolphins with 46 points. They tried to play him man-to-man, and McDaniels missed only nine of his 29 field-goal attempts. Gilmore called McDaniels the best big man—and player—he'd faced. When they met to open the NCAA Tournament at Notre Dame, McDaniels had a tougher time, but his 23 points outdid Gilmore's 12 and the Hilltoppers squeezed out a two-point victory.

His 35 points and 11 rebounds buried Kentucky, the imposing big-brother power from up the road in Lexington that never before had faced Western. Including the consolation victory over Kansas, he averaged 29.4 points in five tournament games. It took Villanova two overtimes—and McDaniels fouling out—to end Western's dream of playing UCLA for the national championship.

A big man from a small town, McDaniels had grown up hoping to attend Western Kentucky. It was a program coach Ed Diddle had built to considerable success, if not quite national renown. His successor, Johnny Oldham, coached the team to NCAA appearances in the two years before McDaniels enrolled, but the 7-footer's tournament play lifted the Hilltoppers toward college basketball's summit.

*Born: April 2, 1948, Scottsville, Ky.*

*The face-up jumper that made McDaniels an offensive force was developed as a teenager, when he was so much taller than the kids he faced on play-grounds that they surrounded the basket and refused to let him approach.*

## CAREER STATS

Career Pts: **2,238**

Scoring Avg: **27.6**

Rebounds Avg: **13.8**

Field Goal %: **.530**

### TOURNAMENT PLAY
**NCAA: 1970, 1971 (3-2)**

**NCAA Final Four: 1971**

### AWARDS AND ACHIEVEMENTS
**Consensus All-American, 1971**

Height/Weight: *7-0/220*　　High School: *Allen County High, Kentucky*　　College: *Western Kentucky University, 1968-1971*

# 74 David ROBINSON

## CAREER STATS

**Career Pts: 2,669**

**Scoring Avg: 21.0**

**Rebounding Avg: 10.3**

**Blocks Avg: 5.24**

**TOURNAMENT PLAY**
NCAA: 1985, 1986, 1987 (4-3)

**AWARDS AND ACHIEVEMENTS**
Robertson Trophy, Naismith Award, Wooden Award, 1987

Consensus
All-American, 1987

*Born: Aug. 6, 1965, Key West, Fla.    Height/Weight: 7-1/240    High School: Osbourn Park High, Manassas, Va.*

## When Robinson finished growing, he stood 7-1, but he had sacrificed little of the quickness and jumping ability that made him appealing as a small-forward prospect.

The secret of David Robinson was out when he completed his second year at Navy. He was a future All-American, a certain pro. He also was clear to leave the academy without owing military service. He chose to stay, becoming an officer and a champion.

With Robinson at center and averaging 27.5 points and 11.8 rebounds, the Midshipmen won three 1985 NCAA Tournament games to reach the East Region final.

"It was a great accomplishment, especially at the Academy," said Paul Evans, the coach of that team. "It was such a great group of guys, and David put the final touches on it."

The Navy coaches did not dream big when they attracted Robinson. They figured if he worked, he might build a career similar to that of Johnny Newman, who starred at Colonial Athletic Association rival Richmond and later played in the NBA. They never imagined they were signing the next great college center.

"It happened fairly quickly," Evans said. "He was 6-7 when we recruited him, but he came into school at 6-9, and he picked up the rest of it during his freshman year." When Robinson finished growing, he stood 7-1, but he had sacrificed little of the quickness and jumping ability that made him appealing as a small-forward prospect.

The reconfigured Robinson was a complete package of basketball possibilities. Because he hadn't been widely recruited, because Navy played in a lesser conference, Robinson's progress was widely interpreted as the work of a tall man against small competition. "David was still learning. People still had their doubts about him," Evans said. "But he was awfully athletic and awfully smart, so he didn't do many stupid things."

Those doubts were obliterated when Robinson played his first NCAA Tournament game, against fourth-seeded LSU in the 1985 opening round. He scored 18 points and grabbed 18 rebounds. Navy won by 23. He never again failed to score 20 points in an NCAA Tournament game. In his final game as a collegian, a first-round loss to Michigan in 1987, Robinson scored 50 of Navy's 82 points. He left no doubt who he was and what he was capable of doing.

*College: U.S. Naval Academy, 1983-1987*

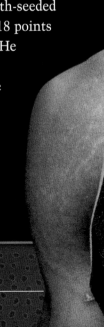

# 75 mateen CLEAVES

The people surrounding him had years of higher education to their credit, prominence in their community and important jobs, but even in this group Mateen Cleaves was in charge.

His sprained ankle commanded the attention of Michigan State's team physician and trainer, but Cleaves' mind was on the 2000 NCAA championship game going on without him. When he limped off the floor after a curious collision with Florida guard Teddy Dupay, the Spartans were ahead by six points and more than 16 minutes remained in the game. Sequestered in the MSU locker room as he received medical attention, he had no idea what was going on in the game.

He knew only this: "They were going to have to amputate my leg to keep me out."

Cleaves returned in time to help Michigan State complete a 13-point victory over Florida and claim its second national championship. Rarely a big scorer, he wounded the Gators with 18 points in the title game. Never a spectacular shooter, he nailed three of his four 3-point attempts.

What made Cleaves an extraordinary college point guard were his command of the game, infectious personality, uncommon strength, physical defense and devotion to team success. He was his own sternest critic, pushing himself to excel in order to carry the Spartans along. His teams compiled a 104-32 record and earned three Big Ten championships.

Bothered by a back injury as a freshman, Cleaves struggled to adjust to college. When he began his sophomore season in full health, he commenced dominating the games he played. He would routinely control the ball through 30 seconds of a possession before finding the opening he wanted and making a play. But he also pushed the ball rapidly upcourt to feed teammates for fastbreak scores.

Always, he was a study in control.

"Everybody said Mateen would turn pro after his junior year," said his Michigan State coach, Tom Izzo. "He was MVP of the league, we'd made the Final Four. I kept saying, 'Are we going to talk about this?' And he'd say, 'I'm not going anywhere.' All he cares about is winning."

*Born: Sept. 7, 1977, Flint, Mich.*

## "They were going to have to amputate my leg to keep me out."

### — Mateen Cleaves

## CAREER STATS

**Career Pts: 1,541**

**Scoring Avg: 12.5**

**TOURNAMENT PLAY**
**NCAA: 1998, 1999, 2000 (12-2)**

**Final Four: 1999, 2000**

**NCAA Champion: 2000**

**AWARDS AND ACHIEVEMENTS**
**NCAA Tournament Most Outstanding Player, 2000**

**Sporting News All-American First Team, 2000**

**Consensus All-American First Team, 1999**

**U.S. Basketball Writers All-American First Team, 1998**

### Why #75?

*Some outsiders wonder how good Cleaves was, but MSU coaches consider him the best program leader they could imagine. He wasn't a shooter, but he made big shots. His impact on defense and as a rebounder should not be ignored.*

**Height/Weight: 6-3/210   High School: Northern High, Flint   College: Michigan State University, 1996-2000**

# 76 Sidney MONCRIEF

**A**rkansas was down to just one Triplet by the time the 1978-79 season commenced. Marvin Delph and Ron Brewer completed their careers the previous March with the Razorbacks' third trip to the Final Four in NCAA Tournament history. Only Sidney Moncrief remained to carry the legacy the trio created.

When the reformulated Razorbacks reached the 1979 Midwest Region final in Cincinnati, they were 25-4. Their opponent, Indiana State, featured 6-9 All-American Larry Bird and entered the game with an unbeaten record. Moncrief came close to spoiling that mark on his own.

When none of the Arkansas big men could contain Bird—he had 27 points through the first 31 minutes—coach Eddie Sutton asked Moncrief to accept the challenge. Bird scored only four more points. When Indiana State tried to break a tie in the final seconds by setting up Bird, Moncrief would not let him near the ball. Instead, Bob Heaton beat the buzzer and the Razorbacks with the Sycamores' last shot.

"It was one of the great games ever," Sutton said. "That was a game you could really see the way Sidney reacted in accepting a challenge. I used the word "stopper" with him ... And he took that as a challenge."

The Triplets essentially created Arkansas basketball. There were four NCAA Tournament appearances before they enrolled and 22 in the years that followed. They were called the Triplets because they stood about the same height, 6-3 or 6-4, and owned similar builds and athletic ability. All were in-state products, and they gave Arkansas a versatile and lethal perimeter attack.

Brewer was the natural playmaker. Delph was the long-distance shooter. "Sidney could play anywhere," Sutton said. With Moncrief's speed, he could score and defend on the wings. With his leaping ability, he was devastating along the baseline. He was not an artful jumpshooter, but he chose his shots wisely and led the nation in field-goal percentage (.665) as a freshman in 1976.

"Sidney, of all the players I ever coached, maximized his God-given talent better than anyone," Sutton said. "He made everybody else on the team play better just because of the work habits he had, the way he played. He could never get enough."

**Born: Sept. 21, 1957, Little Rock, Ark.**

*"Sidney, of all the players I ever coached, maximized his God-given talent better than anyone. He made everybody else on the team play better ..."*

—Coach Eddie Sutton

## CAREER STATS

**Career Pts:** 2,066

**Scoring Avg:** 16.9

**Rebounding Avg:** 8.3

**Field Goal %:** .606

### TOURNAMENT PLAY
**NCAA:** 1977, 1978, 1979, (5-3)

**NCAA Final Four:** 1978

### AWARDS AND ACHIEVEMENTS
**Consensus All-American, 1979**

**Height/Weight:** *6-3/180*    **High School:** *Hall High, Little Rock*    **College:** *University of Arkansas, 1975-1979*

# 77 Terry DISCHINGER

Purdue's Terry Dischinger was set to play his last college game. As had been the case his first two seasons, there would be no NCAA Tournament appearance because Ohio State's absurdly powerful Buckeyes claimed the Big Ten Conference's only bid. A trip to the NIT was out. The league prohibited its teams to play in Madison Square Garden because of repeated work by New York gamblers to fix college games.

There was one distinction Dischinger still could achieve: leading the Big Ten in scoring three consecutive seasons. He was competing against Indiana guard Jimmy Rayl. The Hoosiers-Boilermakers rivalry intensified their duel. Purdue's final game was against Michigan. Indiana was visiting Ohio State. Before he played, Dischinger received a telegram from the Ohio State players, who had grown to respect his class and sportsmanship. It said this: "Go out and get your points. We'll take care of Rayl." Dischinger scored the game-winning basket to defeat the Wolverines and wound up at 30.3 points per game. Rayl finished at 29.8.

"That was the greatest compliment I ever received," Dischinger said. "The fact they respected me enough they would do that—I just thought that was very special."

He played center at only 6-7, but his 14.3 rebounds per game as a sophomore set a Purdue record. He was such a versatile offensive player he changed his game to cope with whatever defensive tactic he faced. Bigger players, such as Indiana's 6-11 Walt Bellamy, were forced to leave the lane to discourage Dischinger from firing jump shots. If they approached too closely, Dischinger could drive the ball and pick up layups or fouls.

He set a Big Ten single-game record with 52 points, making 19-of-28 shots from the field. He was most proud that despite a career 28.3 scoring average, he averaged only 16.4 shots. Nearly a third of his points came at the free-throw line, where he was an 82-percent shooter.

"When I played, I tried to prepare the best I could, studied what I could do and what the teams did," Dischinger said. "Leading the Big Ten in scoring ... it wasn't what I set out to do. It was just the way it happened."

## CAREER STATS

**Career Pts: 1,979**

**Scoring Avg: 28.3**

**Rebounding Avg: 13.7**

**Field Goal %: .553**

## AWARDS AND ACHIEVEMENTS

**Consensus All-American, 1962**

**Consensus All-American, 1961**

*Born: Nov. 21, 1940, Terre Haute, Ind.   Height/Weight: 6-7/189   High School: Garfield High, Terre Haute   College: Purdue University, 1959-62*

# Johnny DAWKINS 78

H e twice was an All-American, was voted the Naismith Award as the top college player, competed in an NCAA championship game and established the career scoring record at a program that has produced eight national players of the year. Nothing Johnny Dawkins accomplished, though, was as important as helping to restore Duke to a position among the elite programs.

The Blue Devils hadn't been away long. They reached the NCAA title game in 1978, four years before Dawkins enrolled, but that was a brief flash of success in a program that had lost its relevance. From 1971 through 1983, the Blue Devils finished at or below .500 six times. Dawkins, who played for the last of those teams, was coach Mike Krzyzewski's most important recruit in helping to escape that malaise. Beginning with Dawkins' senior season in 1986, Duke has appeared nine times in the Final Four.

"Johnny basically put us in a position to win a national title," Krzyzewski said. "His play made me more confident as a coach. With Johnny, I found the ability to be much more aggressive, both offensively and defensively. He's the first player I really gave a green light."

Dawkins made the best use of it. He averaged 25.5 points in Duke's six NCAA Tournament games in 1986, including 24 points in a thrilling semifinal victory over Kansas and 24 points in the championship-game loss to Louisville. He shot 21-of-36 from the field at the Final Four. He never changed expressions whether a game was a comfortable blowout or an excruciating challenge. His clear sense of calm explained his progression from a 79-percent career free-throw shooter to an 88-percent shooter when the game reached the last four four minutes.

Amazingly, Dawkins scored in double figures in 129 of his 133 career games. Although he had a point guard's height, he functioned primarily as a shooting guard. He used his quickness and leaping ability to soar past opponents for baskets in the lane. He launched his lefthanded jumpshot from high above the court.

"Athletically, no one could jump as high as Johnny," Krzyzewski said. "He was spectacular."

## CAREER STATS

**Career Pts: 2,556**

**Scoring Avg: 19.2**

**Rebounding Avg: 4.0**

**Assists: 4.2**

**TOURNAMENT PLAY**
**NCAA: 1984, 1985, 1986 (6-3)**

**AWARDS AND ACHIEVEMENTS**
**Naismith Award, 1986**

**Consensus All-American, 1986**

**Consensus All-American, 1985**

*Born: Sept. 28, 1963, Washington, D.C.   Height/Weight: 6-2/165   High School: Mackin High, Washington   College: Duke University, 1982-1986*

# 79 Lionel SIMMONS

## CAREER STATS

**Career Pts: 3,217**

**Scoring Avg: 24.6**

**Rebounding Avg: 10.9**

**Field Goal %: .501**

**TOURNAMENT PLAY**
**NCAA: 1988, 1989, 1990 (1-3)**

**NIT: 1987**

**AWARDS AND ACHIEVEMENTS**
**Robertson Trophy, Naismith Award, Wooden Award, 1990**

**Consensus All-American, 1990**

*Born: Nov. 14, 1968, Philadelphia*

## Simmons scored points in areas unexplored by most of his contemporaries: the high post, the center of the lane, the short corners.

Watching Lionel Simmons unleash the measured brilliance of his senior season at the Philadelphia Civic Center was like watching the Rolling Stones deliver a concert in a half-empty junior high cafeteria.

Simmons' play was pitch-perfect, and he was ably supported by such teammates as Jack Hurd, Doug Overton and Randy Woods. But the venue was all wrong—dim and ill-suited for Division I basketball—and the performance merited a wider audience. Largely unappreciated as a prep player, Simmons wound up signing at LaSalle when the Explorers competed in the glamour-free Metro Atlantic Athletic Conference. He compensated by succeeding at such an extreme level he could not be ignored.

In more than 30 years of presenting the Naismith Award, the Atlanta Tip-Off Club has honored only three players whose programs operated at the mid-major level: Indiana State's Larry Bird in 1979, Navy's David Robinson in 1987 and Simmons in 1990.

Simmons scored points in areas unexplored by most of his contemporaries: the high post, the center of the lane, the short corners. He was efficient and resourceful. He fearlessly operated inside against bigger and stronger players. In four seasons, Simmons scored 3,217 points. Only two players in the century-plus history of college basketball finished with higher totals: Pete Maravich of LSU with 3,667 and Freeman Williams of Portland State with 3,249.

LaSalle went undefeated in Philadelphia's Big Five in 1989-90, lending credibility to its imposing 29-1 record. But the NCAA selection committee did not treat the Explorers gently. They were seeded only fourth in the East Region and faced a second-round game against Clemson, which featured future NBA big men Elden Campbell and Dale Davis.

The only consolation was the site: the Hartford Civic Center, an easy trip for Philadelphia fans. After building a 16-point halftime lead, LaSalle was worn down by Clemson's overwhelming size and eventually fell behind to stay. Simmons fouled out inside the final minute, having scored 28 points in his last college game. There were plenty of Explorers fans to applaud him for a career filled with quiet achievement, but their ovation spread to include most of the 15,000 in attendance. Finally, Simmons had an audience worthy of his talent.

*Height/Weight:* **6-7/210** *High School:* **Southern High, Philadelphia** *College:* **LaSalle University, 1986-1990**

# 80 Bailey HOWELL

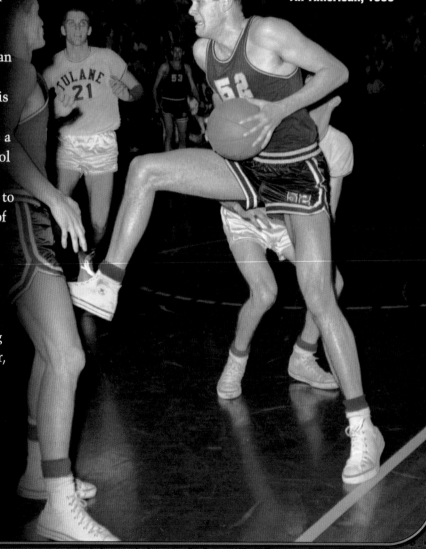

H e is the man who broke the Southeastern Conference scoring record set by the great Bob Pettit. He ranked among the nation's top 10 in scoring and rebounding in all three years of his varsity career. He led the NCAA in field-goal percentage as a sophomore and helped build Mississippi State's program toward a reign of power in a league perennially ruled by Kentucky. Bailey Howell also may be the greatest player during the NCAA Tournament era to be excluded from postseason play.

As a senior in 1959, he averaged 27.5 points and the Maroons soared to 24-1 and No. 3 in the polls—but state officials prohibited them to play integrated teams in the NCAAs.

Howell ended his career with a win over Mississippi, and that victory meant a lot to him. He never cared for the Rebels while growing up a Tennessee Vols football fan in tiny Middleton, about 85 miles east of Memphis. He declined recruiting interest from Adoph Rupp because Kentucky was too far from home. He chose Mississippi State because Starkville's small-town atmosphere suited him.

From the start of his varsity career, Howell was an inside scoring force. Mississippi State had not been more than a game over .500 in a dozen years, but his 25.9 points per game and NCAA-best 57-percent shooting helped produced a 17-8 record. He became a second-team All-American as a junior and the school achieved its first 20-win season.

Howell regularly triumphed over zones designed to stop him. He also had to deal with stalling tactics of his coach, Babe McCarthy, who greedily protected leads. "It wasn't a lot of fun to play that way," Howell said, "but we won with it."

Howell retired to Starkville from an NBA career that gained him entry to the Naismith Memorial Basketball Hall of Fame. When introduced to young Mississippi State fans as the school's greatest player, Howell said they'll ask, "How did y'all do in the N-C-double-A?"

When he tells them, "They're dumbfounded. They can't even believe it happened. It's just so unbelievable. It was just ridiculous." Howell will be best remembered for the games he did play. It's a shame there weren't more.

## CAREER STATS

**Career Pts: 2,030**

**Scoring Avg: 27.1**

**Rebounding Avg: 17.0**

**Field Goal %: .525**

## AWARDS AND ACHIEVEMENTS
**Consensus All-American, 1959**

---

**Born:** Jan. 20, 1937, Middleton, Tenn.     **Height/Weight:** 6-7/220     **High School:** Middleton High     **College:** Mississippi State University, 1956-1959

# Bo LAMAR

## 81

The floating, arcing, rainbow jumper that made a shooting star of Dwight "Bo" Lamar was the product of science, not art. He was a scrawny kid playing ball as a pre-teen on the streets of Columbus, Ohio, often against high school students. "It was out of necessity," Lamar said. "They were blocking my shots, and I got tired of it."

He grew as his college career at Southwestern Louisiana approached, and his legend burgeoned as he became the only player to lead the NCAA's college division and university division in scoring.

The 3,493 points Lamar scored from 1969 through 1973 would rank second in NCAA history—if nearly half the points had not been accumulated while the Ragin' Cajuns were classified a small-college program. Thus the NCAA's career scoring list jumps directly from Pete Maravich (3,667) to Freeman Williams (3,249).

"I had a coach early in my career tell me, 'If you're good enough, you don't have to say it,' " Lamar said. "The main thing is, we won. I don't know many leading scorers who won like we did."

Southwestern Louisiana stepped forward in class in 1971-72, but this did not cause Lamar or his team to decline. In his final two seasons, the Cajuns were 49-9, ranked in the top 10 and reached the NCAA Tournament round of 16. In 1972, Lamar led the NCAA's top division with his 36.3 scoring average. In the 30 years since, only Loyola Marymount's Bo Kimble and Purdue's Glenn Robinson won the scoring title and also reached the Sweet 16. Lamar's prolific scoring became his trademark, but he was a disruptive defender adept at stealing the ball and a productive passer credited with 5.1 assists per game as a senior.

Lamar was largely overlooked in high school, even though there were plenty of chances to see him for coaches scouting his teammate, future Long Beach State All-American Ed Ratleff. Ratleff tried to talk 49ers coach Jerry Tarkanian into signing Lamar. Tarkanian told Ratleff he merely wanted a friend on the team. "After I led the nation in scoring, a lot of the coaches in Ohio tried to say they recruited me," Lamar said. "They lied."

## CAREER STATS

**Career Pts: 1,862**

**Scoring Avg: 32.7**

**Assists Avg: 4.8**

**Field Goal %: .454**

### TOURNAMENT PLAY
**NCAA: 1972, 1973 (2-2)**

### AWARDS AND ACHIEVEMENTS
**Consensus All-American, 1973**

**Consensus All-American, 1972**

**Born:** April 7, 1951, Columbus, Ohio    **Height/Weight:** 6-1/175
**High School:** East High, Columbus    **College:** University of Southwestern Louisiana, 1969-1973

153    Legends of College Basketball

# 82 Guy RODGERS

Philadelphia basketball was introduced to its enduringly popular Big Five competition in 1956, the same year Temple's Guy Rodgers entered the college game. Many believe the city hasn't seen a better player since.

When the *Philadelphia Daily News* conducted a readers poll in 1981 to name the greatest player in the Big Five—which comprises Temple, Villanova, St. Joseph's, Penn and LaSalle—Rodgers won by a wide margin. He was a charter member of the Big Five Hall of Fame. Rodgers represented everything a Philadelphia fan loves in a guard: tough, clever, unselfish, versatile, committed to his team—and a hometown guy.

So great a star at Northeast High that he won the city scoring championship away from Wilt Chamberlain, Rodgers teamed with shooting guard Hal Lear to give Temple a backcourt that ranks with the very best: Gail Goodrich/Walt Hazzard at UCLA, Jerry Eaves/Darrell Griffith at Louisville, Bobby Wilkerson/Quinn Buckner at Indiana.

Rodgers was a rugged lefty who thrived on overpowering defenders. He was not a great outside shooter, but he compensated with quickness that allowed him to penetrate and a knack for impossible passes that generated scoring opportunities. With Temple, often that meant scoring opportunities for teammates as well as himself. Rodgers was good for 18.8 points and 8.0 assists as the Owls reached the 1956 Final Four before losing to Iowa in the semifinals. Lear averaged 28 points in the tournament. He frequently credited Rodgers with supplying him the passes necessary to score big.

As a senior, Rodgers was without the company of Lear in the backcourt but managed beautifully. With Rodgers the top scorer and offensive leader, the Owls had won 25 consecutive games and held the No. 5 ranking entering the Final Four. They owned a 4-point lead with 90 seconds remaining of a semifinal game against Kentucky, but a charging call against Temple's Bill Kennedy and a missed free throw by Rodgers—and a pro-UK crowd in Louisville—facilitated the Wildcats' comeback.

However costly, it was a rare mistake in a spectacular career. Many times, Temple coach Harry Litwack was quoted as saying Rodgers was the best player he ever coached. One missed shot could not change that.

*Born: Sept. 1, 1935, Philadelphia    Died: Feb. 19, 2001*

# In 1956, Temple's Guy Rodgers entered the college game. Many believe the city of Philadelphia hasn't seen a better player since.

## CAREER STATS

Career Pts: **1,767**

Scoring Avg: **19.6**

Rebounding Avg: **6.5**

Field Goal %: **.421**

### TOURNAMENT PLAY
NCAA: 1956, 1958
(5-2)

NCAA Final Four:
1956, 1958

NIT: 1957

### AWARDS AND ACHIEVEMENTS
Consensus
All-American, 1958

*Height/Weight: 6-0/180    High School: Northeast High, Philadelphia    College: Temple University, 1955-1958*

# 83 Art HEYMAN

If Art Heyman had not been a national player of the year, an All-American, a three-time All-Atlantic Coast Conference selection and the scoring force at the heart of Duke's first Final Four team, he probably would have been revered by Blue Devils fans merely for brawling with the North Carolina Tar Heels.

Heyman had been recruited by North Carolina but turned down the Tar Heels to join coach Vic Bubas at Duke, which led to the program's first sustained period of success. So Heyman had come early to the Duke-North Carolina rivalry, the greatest in the sport given the two programs' achievements and their separation by eight miles on highway 15/501.

When the teams met in February 1961, the 17th game of his first varsity season, Heyman tangled with Carolina guard Larry Brown, a familiar opponent from their days playing high school ball on Long Island. The scuffle that ensued put Heyman opposite a UNC male cheerleader, as well. It went so far that afterward an attorney who was a Tar Heel fan tried to have Heyman arrested.

Heyman should be respected for his basketball skills rather than that incident, but it did illustrate his feisty competitiveness. Heyman was a small forward so polished he was co-captain as a sophomore and an integral part of a 22-6 team. Duke averaged 15 victories in the four years before his debut.

As Bubas attracted talented players including guard Jeff Mullins and center Jay Buckley, Heyman's statistics declined slightly but the team progressed. In his senior year, the Blue Devils dropped just two December games—by five total points—and entered the NCAA Tournament riding an 18-game winning streak. The Devils fell in the semifinals at the Final Four to eventual champion Loyola of Chicago, but Heyman's 51 points and 19 rebounds in his final two games earned him recognition as the tournament's most outstanding player.

It was a glorious end to his career, but he could just as easily have quit following his final regular-season home game. On Feb. 28, 1963, Duke beat North Carolina, 106-93, a result that gave him a 5-2 career record against the Tar Heels. Heyman scored 40 points. This was tough to top.

## CAREER STATS

**Career Pts:** 1,984    **Scoring Avg:** 25.1
**Rebounding Avg:** 10.9    **Field Goal %:** .451
**TOURNAMENT PLAY:** NCAA: 1963    NCAA Final Four: 1963
**AWARDS AND ACHIEVEMENTS:** Oscar Robertson Trophy, 1963
NCAA Tournament Most Outstanding Player, 1963
Consensus All-American, 1963

**Born:** June 24, 1941, Rockville Center, N.Y.    **Height/Weight:** 6-5/205    **High School:** Oceanside High    **College:** Duke University, 1960-1963

# Chet WALKER 84

The *Peoria Journal Star*'s advance story on the opening game of Bradley's 1959-60 season waited 14 paragraphs before mentioning Chet Walker's name. "It is hoped that 6-6 Chester Walker will become a major scorer and rebounder," wrote sportswriter Max Seibel. That hope was fulfilled within 24 hours. Walker's performance screamed from the headlines of the following day's paper.

His debut with the Bradley varsity was a 44-point, school-record performance that also included 13 rebounds. He left the victory over Abilene Christian with more than 12 minutes to play. The Braves had added the remaining element of what would become a championship team. They claimed the 1960 NIT title with three victories by double-digit margins. Walker, who averaged 21.8 points, struggled in the championship game against Providence and was on the bench as Bradley faced a 12-point deficit. He asked to return. Teammate Dan Smith said afterward, "That was the inspiration to us." Walker was effective in the full-court press as the Braves scored 38 points in the final 10 minutes to win by 16.

Bradley ranked no lower than No. 6 in the polls during Walker's career. The Braves did not reach the NCAA Tournament because they shared the Missouri Valley Conference with powerhouse Cincinnati, which earned the champion's automatic berth all three years. However, Walker scored 28 points in a 91-90 upset of Cincinnati as a sophomore. Bradley defeated the Bearcats once in each of his seasons—three of their seven losses in that period.

Walker grew both in stature and status during his last two seasons at Bradley, adding an inch in height and All-American honors both years.

Chet "the Jet" was a smooth player who functioned at once as a power forward and small forward. He could control the boards with his strength and grit and generate points with his shooting and quickness. He sliced through defenses for layups and dunks, like the one with 40 seconds left in that 1960 victory over Cincinnati that gave Bradley the lead for good.

His Bradley career closed in 1962 with a first-round NIT loss to Duquesne, but Walker contributed 27 points and 13 rebounds that nearly averted defeat. From beginning to end, his play was newsworthy.

## CAREER STATS

Career Pts: **1,975**  Scoring Avg: **24.4**
Rebounding Avg: **12.8**  Field Goal %: **.552**
TOURNAMENT PLAY: **NIT: 1960, 1962**  **NIT Champion: 1960**
AWARDS AND ACHIEVEMENTS: **Consensus All-American, 1962**
**Consensus All-American, 1961**

*Born: Feb. 22, 1940, Benton Harbor, Mich.   Height/Weight: 6-7/210   High School: Benton Harbor High   College: Bradley University, 1959-1962*

# 85 Juan DIXON

It's doubtful any legend came from humbler beginnings than Juan Dixon. His parents were drug abusers who died of AIDS while Dixon was a teenager. He was raised by his brother and extended family. As a high school player, Dixon did not carry a can't-miss reputation. There wasn't much he could carry. He weighed 140 pounds when he arrived at Maryland.

"A lot of people counted me out before I even got here," Dixon said. "Not having my parents around, it was a little harder. But I stayed strong."

Gary Williams, Dixon's coach, saw something special in this skinny shooter. Scouting a summer tournament game in a sweltering gym, Williams noticed Dixon hustling at the end of a long day. "Juan was the one guy on the court still diving, still trying to do whatever he could to help his team," Williams said. "Sometimes you play a hunch in recruiting and it works out OK."

In a short while, that quality was obvious to everyone. After backing up All-American Steve Francis as a freshman, Dixon emerged as an 18-point scorer and All-Atlantic Coast Conference player. Dixon finished as the second Maryland player named All-ACC three times and the school's career scoring leader.

Dixon did not have the size or athletic gifts of some shooting guard contemporaries, and his jumper wasn't unfailingly accurate. He was a relentless worker without the ball, however, and particularly dangerous after sliding from behind a screen. Dixon picked up hundreds of points by stealing the ball and rushing to complete layups. His 333 steals ranked 10th in NCAA history.

His most important statistical achievements were his 155 points in the 2002 NCAA Tournament and 294 career tournament points, each ranking him ninth on the all-time list. Those points were the principal reason Maryland earned its first Final Four berth in 2001 and followed that a year later with an NCAA championship.

At the end of the title-game victory over Indiana, having scored 18 points after battling through exceptional defense from Hoosiers guard Dane Fife, Dixon raised his arms in triumph. A tattoo on one of them said this: Only The Strong Survive.

*Born: Oct. 9, 1978, Baltimore, Md.    Height/Weight: 6-3/164    High School: Calvert Hall High    College: University of Maryland, 1998-2002*

**"Juan was the one guy on the court still diving, still trying to do whatever he could to help his team."**

—Gary Williams

## CAREER STATS

**Career Pts: 2,269**

**Scoring Avg: 16.1**

**3-Point %: .389**

**Steals Avg: 2.4**

**TOURNAMENT PLAY**
**NCAA: 1999, 2000, 2001, 2002 (13-3)**

**NCAA Final Four: 2001, 2002**

**NCAA Champion: 2002**

**AWARDS AND ACHIEVEMENTS**
**Consensus All-American, 2002**

**NCAA Tournament Most Outstanding Player, 2002**

# 86 Doug COLLINS

## CAREER STATS

**Career Pts: 2,240**

**Scoring Avg: 29.1**

**Rebounding Avg: 5.5**

**Field Goal %: .476**

## AWARDS AND ACHIEVEMENTS
**Consensus
All-American, 1973**

*Born: July 28, 1951, Christopher, Ill.*

> ## "My junior year, I was the guy from Illinois State. My senior year, I was the guy who played on the Olympic team."
> — Doug Collins

Outside of his immediate family and some Illinois State fans, not many people knew of Doug Collins when the summer of 1972 commenced. When it concluded, he was as widely known as any player this side of Bill Walton.

Collins played for the U.S. Olympic team that summer, the team that lost the gold medal game to the Soviet Union in controversial fashion. Collins was the team's best player, with the stamina to outrun smaller guards and a gift for scoring from anywhere on the offensive end. He returned to Illinois State with an All-American reputation. His scoring output declined more than six points from his stellar junior season, when he averaged 32.6, but he made most All-American teams, anyway.

"That's sort of the way things work in this business," Collins said. "Once people know who you are, they look at you differently. My junior year, I was the guy from Illinois State. My senior year, I was the guy who played on the Olympic team."

Collins attributed his senior-year slide to exhaustion from competing in the Olympics. He had no time to rest in the summer. The Games that year were in September, so he went directly from the gold-medal defeat to resuming school and preseason conditioning at Illinois State. It isn't like he needs to apologize, though, for a season in which he averaged 26 points and shot 47.6 percent from the field.

As a junior in high school, Collins was not good enough to start for his varsity team, but he grew six inches through the course of his senior year and continued to develop his skill level. Collins became the first Division I scholarship player at Illinois State and played for the NCAA's first African-American coach at that level, Will Robinson. Collins' three seasons were the Redbirds' first after stepping up in competition, and they achieved winning seasons in each of those years.

"I couldn't wait to get into the gym every day," Collins said. "I was growing, I was getting bigger, I was getting better. The game was fun. I couldn't imagine a young guy being able to have that kind of fun."

**Height/Weight:** 6-6/170   **High School:** Benton (Ill.) High   **College:** Illinois State University, 1970-1973

# 87 Julius ERVING

hen coach Jack Leaman stumbled onto Julius Erving while scouting a center prospect playing in the same high school game, he found himself enthralled with this 6-2 guard who owned great hands and an appetite for hard work. When Erving arrived at Massachusetts, he was four inches taller and grabbed 26 rebounds in a freshman game. "That was the end of that guard stuff," Leaman said. It soon was the end of that Julius stuff, also. Here, Erving became Dr. J.

He was occasionally discouraged by the lack of competition, and it prevented him from gaining recognition. He never rose higher than third-team All-American. The school's small gym made it hard to attract elite opponents. But eager fans lined up outside the Curry Hicks Cage hours in advance of games. He never disappointed. In two seasons, Erving scored in double figures in every game. With hands so large they could swallow a basketball whole, he grabbed double-figure rebounds in each game but his last. Erving finished his career as one of six players to average more than 20 points and 20 rebounds.

"The best thing for Julius was he learned the game as a small person, then grew into his body and became a big guy with little-guy skills," Leaman said. "He just seemed to know the game more than anybody else."

Erving's production was not simply a matter of playing overmatched opponents. His sophomore debut consisted of 27 points and 28 rebounds against New England power Providence. Erving's greatest game was against Syracuse, when he burned the Orangemen with 36 points and 32 rebounds.

He was among the first players to lift the game off the floor and above the rim. The dunk was illegal during his two seasons, so he could not make use of what would become his signature as a professional, but Erving still was able to climb higher to grab rebounds and drop in layups than his opponents could ever conceive.

"The two years that he played, he couldn't use that ability to dunk the ball," Leaman said. "We never really saw him put on a show the way he could put it down."

**Born: Feb. 22, 1950, Roosevelt, N.Y.**

> *"The best thing for Julius was he learned the game as a small person, then grew into his body and became a big guy with little-guy skills."*
>
> — Jack Leaman

## CAREER STATS

Career Pts: **1,370**

Scoring Avg: **26.3**

Rebounding Avg: **20.2**

Field Goal %: **.487**

## TOURNAMENT PLAY
**NIT 1970, 1971 (0-2)**

*Height/Weight:* **6-6/205**   *High School:* **Roosevelt High**   *College:* **University of Massachusetts, 1969-1971**

# 88 Corliss WILLIAMSON

Corliss Williamson might have been the smallest big man who ever ruled the college game. At least an inch shorter than his listed 6-6 height—and far smaller than the players he dominated inside—Williamson was the most consistently successful low-post player of the 1990s.

In a period when most players his size were working to become Michael Jordan-style shooting guards, Williamson developed the ability to position himself near the baseline and used his footwork, strength and quickness to power through opponents for baskets. In 91 college games, he attempted 1,127 shots. Only six were 3-point tries.

" 'The Big Nasty' is every coach's dream," said Nolan Richardson, Williamson's coach at Arkansas. But that wasn't exactly right. He was Richardson's dream, because only he got to work with him.

Richardson was building the Arkansas program toward national-power status when he encountered the good fortune of having Williamson grow up two hours from campus. The state produces few star basketball players. His decision to stay at home and play for the Razorbacks led to their most glorious period.

In Williamson's three years, Arkansas compiled an 85-19 record and reached two NCAA championship games, defeating Duke in 1994 for the Razorbacks' first national title. Williamson scored 23 points and got eight rebounds in that game.

It almost was routine for Williamson to produce in the most important games. He became one of eight players to score more than 300 points in the NCAA Tournament, averaging 20.2 per game. Against Southeastern Conference rival Kentucky, the two-time league player of the year scored 20 or more points five times in six games.

Unfortunately, Williamson endured one of his most difficult games in his last outing as a Razorback, a loss to UCLA in the 1995 NCAA title game. As well as some spectators remember that game, it is too easily forgotten that Williamson and his Razorbacks teammates entered on an 11-game NCAA Tournament winning streak. He was bothered by the size of 7-foot UCLA center George Zidek and shot 3-of-16 from the field. It was one of the few days he wasn't quite big enough to be a champion.

*Born: Dec. 4, 1973, Russellville, Ark.*

**" 'The Big Nasty' is every coach's dream."** —Nolan Richardson

## CAREER STATS

**Career Pts: 1,728**

**Scoring Avg: 19.0**

**Rebounding Avg: 7.1**

**Field Goal %: .583**

### TOURNAMENT PLAY
**NCAA: 1993, 1994, 1995 (13-2)**

**NCAA Final Four: 1994, 1995**

**NCAA Champion: 1994**

### AWARDS AND ACHIEVEMENTS
**Sporting News All-American, 1995**

**NCAA Tournament Most Outstanding Player, 1994**

**Height/Weight: 6-6/225    High School: Russellville High    College: University of Arkansas, 1992-1995**

# 89 Marcus CAMBY

The unveiling of Marcus Camby's excellence as the 1995-96 season commenced was as sudden as a summer storm. He was gifted, promising and valuable as a Massachusetts sophomore. The next year, just like that, he was the nation's preeminent player in a season loaded with extraordinary talent: Allen Iverson, Tim Duncan, Ray Allen, Lorenzen Wright.

The reason he hadn't dominated sooner was all too uncommon for the era in which Camby played. As a young player new to college basketball, he deferred to veteran star Lou Roe. "That was Lou's team," said John Calipari, Camby's UMass coach. "Marcus was an unbelievable teammate, very unselfish. He had no issues with anybody else's success. If someone else scored 30, he was happy for them."

In his first two seasons, Camby contented himself with asserting his presence as an interior defender. His shot-blocking helped the Minutemen compile a 57-12 record and win consecutive Atlantic 10 Conference championships, but his minutes were limited as he developed stamina. He barely scored in double figures.

A succession of elite opponents at the outset of his junior year provided the opportunity and impetus for Camby to flourish. His duel with Duncan ended with Camby scoring 17 points, holding Duncan to nine and UMass beating Wake Forest. He scorched Memphis' Wright with corner jumpers and finished with 23 points in a thrilling victory. Most important was the team's season-opening triumph over Kentucky, the preseason No. 1 team, in which Camby overwhelmed the Wildcats with 32 points and helped convince Calipari of his team's potential.

One of the more excitable coaches, Calipari was furiously pacing and shouting instructions as the Minutemen edged toward an unexpected victory. "Marcus runs over to me with about five minutes left," Calipari said, "and he tells me: 'Would you calm down? We're going to win the game. Just relax.'"

UMass carried an unbeaten record 26 games into the season and didn't lose until February 24, 1996. That was its only loss until Kentucky avenged its early season defeat in the national semifinals. The end came too soon for that group of Minutemen, but Camby arrived just in time.

**Born:** March 22, 1974, Hartford, Conn.    **Height/Weight:** 6-11/220    **High School:** Hartford Public High

"Marcus was an unbelievable teammate, very unselfish. He had no issues with anybody else's success. If someone else scored 30, he was happy for them."

—John Calipari

## CAREER STATS

Career Pts: **1,387**

Scoring Avg: **15.1**

Rebounding Avg: **7.0**

Blocks Avg: **3.7**

**TOURNAMENT PLAY**
NCAA: **1994, 1995, 1996 (8-3)**

NCAA Final Four: **1996**

**AWARDS AND ACHIEVEMENTS**
Robertson Trophy, Naismith Award, Wooden Award, 1996

Unanimous All-American, 1996

College: *University of Massachusetts, 1993-1996*

# 90 John LUCAS

The game of basketball almost seemed too easy for John Lucas. Other players, even great players, appeared to be working furiously as they dealt with opponents' talents and tactics. Lucas could score 25 points and pass for six assists and appear as though he'd just rolled off the couch from a hard afternoon of TV-watching.

He was as natural an athlete as anyone who played this sport. Lucas was so gifted he became a championship-level tennis player and competed professionally. He had imposing size for a point guard, a smooth gait that made it difficult for opponents to detect a shift in speed and the advantage of playing lefthanded. He employed what resembled a set shot more than a jumper, probably the last All-American player to use that technique.

Lucas was versatile enough to play any perimeter position, and he spent his final two seasons primarily at shooting guard. Maryland had recruited Brad Davis, an excellent prospect whose skill was as a passer, so coach Lefty Driesell asked Lucas to shoot more often. "But I always thought of myself as a point guard," Lucas said. His assist average dropped in 1974-75, but that team advanced to the NCAA regional finals, the deepest tournament advancement during his career.

That might not have been the case if Maryland had been included in the 1974 tournament, but that was the last year before multiple teams from the same conference were extended invitations. The Terps played NC State in the ACC Tournament championship game and trailed by one point with nine seconds left in overtime when Lucas missed two free throws. The Wolfpack squeezed out a 103-100 victory. "I cried like a baby at the end of that game," he said.

Lucas did not return to Cole Field House often in its final years as Maryland's home. He was disappointed Driesell was forced to leave the program. He had his own affairs to manage as an NBA coach with such teams as the San Antonio Spurs and Cleveland Cavaliers.

"And now that they've closed Cole," Lucas said, "all my history left with the building."

That isn't true, of course. A legend is not so easily erased.

*Born: Oct. 31, 1953, Durham, N.C.*

*He was as natural an athlete as anyone who played this sport.*

## CAREER STATS

Career Pts: **2,015**

Scoring Avg: **18.3**

Assists Avg: **4.7**

Field Goal %: **.525**

### TOURNAMENT PLAY
NCAA: 1973, 1975 (3-2)

### AWARDS AND ACHIEVEMENTS
Consensus All-American, 1976

Consensus All-American, 1975

ht: 6-4/170   High School: Hillside High, Durham   College: University of Maryland, 1972-1976

# 91 Kenyon MARTIN

ntil that moment arrived, with 3:46 on the Allstate Arena clock, it seemed Cincinnati easily would win every Conference USA game in 1999-2000. Fourteen victims had fallen hard. Now, with so little time before the finish, the Bearcats trailed DePaul by 10.

Cincinnati coach Bob Huggins glanced at the Blue Demons in a timeout huddle. "I thought they believed the game was over," Huggins said. "I told our guys: 'Look down there. Look at them!' And I told them whoever shot the ball before Kenyon touched it was never playing again."

This is the image of Kenyon Martin's senior season Huggins wishes to preserve: Martin scoring 10 points in what remained of that game, blocking two shots and assisting on the game-winning basket. Though Martin ruled the sport that winter, he never was more dominant than on that Thursday night in February. And, within a week, his career ended.

That's the memory Huggins prefers to suppress. The Bearcats, ranked No. 1, were nearly four minutes into a conference tournament opener when Martin collided with a Saint Louis player and fell awkwardly, breaking his leg. Martin became the first Wooden Award winner to miss the NCAA Tournament. Without him, Cincinnati lost in the second round. Huggins still insists that team, with a healthy Martin, would have won the championship.

As good as Martin was, that's difficult to dispute. He not only swept the 2000 player of the year trophies, he shared the defensive player of the year award with Duke's Shane Battier.

Martin always had been an elite defender because of his shot-blocking skills, but he was a reluctant shooter his first three seasons. Because he was erratic at the free-throw line, he avoided body contact in the lane. When practice finally cured that disorder, he was ready to star.

Just before his senior year began, Martin sat on the Cincinnati bench and, despite a single-figure career scoring average, boldly suggested he was good enough to win the Wooden Award. Then he proved himself right. That he ended his career on that bench might have cost Cincinnati a third national title but did not diminish Martin's achievements.

**Born: Dec. 30, 1977, Saginaw, Mich.     Height/Weight: 6-9/220     High School: Bryan Adams High, Dallas**

*"I thought they believed the game was over. I told our guys: 'Look down there. Look at them!' And I told them whoever shot the ball before Kenyon touched it was never playing again."*

—Bob Huggins

## Why #91?

Not until his senior year did Kenyon Martin become a transcendent player, but he ranked among the top defenders the previous two seasons. Perhaps only Larry Bird and Glenn Robinson had better seasons in the post-Wooden years.

### CAREER STATS

**Career Pts: 1,279**

**Scoring Avg: 11.0**

**Rebounding Avg: 7.5**

**Blocks Avg: 2.5**

**TOURNAMENT PLAY**
NCAA: 1997, 1998, 1999 (3-3)

**AWARDS AND ACHIEVEMENTS**
Robertson Trophy, Naismith Trophy, Wooden Award, 2000

Unanimous All-American, 2000

NABC Defensive Player of the Year, 2000

*College: University of Cincinnati, 1996-2000*

# 92 Richard HAMILTON

## CAREER STATS

**Career Pts: 2,036**   **Scoring Avg: 19.8**   **Rebounding Avg: 4.5**   **3-pointers: 237-of-627 (.378)**

**TOURNAMENT PLAY:   NIT: 1997     NCAA: 1998, 1999 (9-1)     NCAA Champion: 1999**

**AWARDS AND ACHIEVEMENTS: NCAA Tournament Most Outstanding Player, 1999     Consensus All-American, 1999**

*Born: Feb. 14, 1978, Coatesville, Pa.*

## "All of a sudden it was 'Voila!' He was a player."

—Jim Calhoun

He arrived at Connecticut with a ready-made nickname: Rip. That didn't seem to fit this scrawny teenager who barely weighed 170 pounds and spent many of his early days with the Huskies being mauled by teammates in practice. It turned out the name was borrowed from his father, who became a very proud Rip Sr. by the time Richard Hamilton completed his college career.

In his final game at Connecticut, Hamilton repeatedly lured Duke defenders into solid screens and popped open for mid-range jump shots that helped generate the Huskies' stunning 77-74 NCAA title game victory. Duke entered that game with a 37-1 record and was being discussed as one of the greatest college teams. After Hamilton had punished the Devils with 27 points, they weren't even champions.

"Rip had a great ability to block everything out," said Jim Calhoun, Hamilton's coach at Connecticut. "He got excited in wins, but he never really was impressed by the magnitude of what he did. It wasn't that he was uncaring. He was oblivious at the right time."

Hamilton was a high school star and coveted recruit, but his lack of strength caused him to develop slowly as a freshman. He started every game, but shot less than 40 percent from the field and 35 percent on 3-pointers. The Connecticut coaching staff pushed him to develop and, at the close of the year, was rewarded when Hamilton averaged 25 points in five NIT games. He lifted his season scoring average by nearly two points in that stretch. "All of a sudden," Calhoun said, "it was 'Voila!' He was a player."

Hamilton's slight build created the illusion that he didn't have each game tightly in his grasp, but his knack for fluttering from place to place on offense and finding open space the moment it was created eventually made him only the second UConn player to reach 2,000 career points. He prided himself on being unpredictable, saying there was no single way to defend him. He understood the mechanics of being a scorer.

"He was the only guy I ever had that I wouldn't think was playing well, and he'd have 36 points," Calhoun said. "Scoring was easy."

**Height/Weight:** 6-6/185    **High School:** Coatesville Area High    **College:** University of Connecticut, 1996-1999

# 93 Dean MEMINGER

For a basketball player at the dawn of the 1970s, the fashion of the day called for large Afros and huge numbers under the column labeled "field-goal attempts." All the guys were doing it: Austin Carr, Calvin Murphy, Pete Maravich. None shot less than 26 times per game. None won as often as Dean "The Dream" Meminger.

He arrived at Marquette with a superstar's reputation but not the accompanying attitude. When his contemporaries were firing jumpers at will, Meminger adopted the egalitarian approach to offense that eventually became the norm. He was ahead of his time.

Meminger found satisfaction in passing to teammates. His teams were spectacularly successful, compiling a composite 78-9 record. He controlled the ball so effortlessly coach Al McGuire once called him the best ballhandler who ever lived. He once dribbled away the final minutes of a victory over Notre Dame to prevent the Irish from completing a comeback from 17 points down. With no shot clock to dissuade him, Meminger bounced away the time until the Fighting Irish either grew exhausted and surrendered or became frustrated and fouled.

Meminger didn't sacrifice much by functioning more as a playmaker and defender. He did lead the Warriors in scoring for two straight years. He directed them to 27 consecutive victories as a senior, before they fell by a point to Ohio State in the NCAA Tournament. As a junior, he was most valuable player of the National Invitation Tournament, which Marquette won after declining an NCAA bid because McGuire was unhappy with the bracketing procedures.

Though he did not generate the astonishing numbers of other great guards, Meminger was appreciated. Voters for All-American teams recognized his accomplishments. McGuire still sometimes felt awkward that Meminger did not demand the same offensive freedom as his peers. He wanted there to be at least one time when Meminger would cut loose. It finally arrived in the last home game of his career, a visit from Tulane. Meminger scored 33 points, a career high. The Warriors concluded a perfect regular season that night with their 26th victory. He left little doubt which mattered more.

**Born: May 13, 1948, New York**

## *He arrived at Marquette with a superstar's reputation but not the accompanying attitude.*

**REER STATS**

**eer Pts: 1,637**

**ring Avg: 18.8**

**ounding Avg: 5.1**

**d Goal %: .464**

**URNAMENT PLAY**

**A: 1969, 1971**

**)**

**1970**

**Champion: 1970**

**ARDS AND**
**HIEVEMENTS**

**sensus**
**American, 1971**

**verse**
**American, 1970**

**Most Valuable**
**yer, 1970**

*Height/Weight: 6-0/165    High School: Rice High, New York City    College: Marquette University, 1968-1971*

# 94 Ernie DiGREGORIO

The marriage of Ernie DiGregorio to Providence College basketball in the wild offensive days of the early 1970s could not have been more fortuitous. He was the right player at the right school at the one time in the game's history when his gifts as a point guard could be fully appreciated.

DiGregorio was blessed to play in his hometown, with its large concentration of Italian-Americans elated to celebrate the command, daring and genius he demonstrated on the court. He was not particularly big or fast. He moved quickly with the ball, however, and thought three pages ahead of everyone else in the game.

He played with a sense of wizardry, a flair for creating scoring opportunities that had no right or reason to materialize. His magic was such that even though he attempted 728 shots his senior year, an average of more than 20 per game, he remained best known—and most feared—for his ability to pass the ball.

His masterpiece in that category occurred at the pinnacle of his college career, when the Friars advanced to the 1973 Final Four. They were matched against Memphis in the semifinals and Ernie D detected an opportunity no one else noticed. Gaining possession in the backcourt, he spotted teammate Kevin Stacom streaking toward the goal. DiGregorio did what anyone else might have done, so long as that anyone was named Pete Maravich or Earl Monroe. DiGregorio snapped off a behind-the-pack pass that traveled nearly 50 feet and hit Stacom in stride.

It was a spectacular moment in a game that became a crushing disappointment. Providence was progressing smartly toward a championship meeting against UCLA when star center Marvin Barnes dislocated his knee. The Friars led by nine at halftime but couldn't hold it. Without his most important inside target available, DiGregorio shot 36 times and scored 32 points.

He was not the most oppressive defender—detractors called him Ernie No-D when he reached the NBA—but the sum of his abilities as a leader, creator, passer and scorer made him the best pure offensive point guard to play Division I basketball.

As Stacom later told the *Boston Globe*: "He was the best at making others better."

*Born: Jan. 15, 1951, North Providence, R.I.*

*"He was the best at making others better."*

—Kevin Stacom

## CAREER STATS

**Career Pts: 1,760**

**Scoring Avg: 20.5**

**Assists Avg: 7.7**

**Field Goal %: .468**

### TOURNAMENT PLAY
**NCAA: 1972, 1973 (3-2)**

**NCAA Final Four: 1973**

**NIT: 1971**

### AWARDS AND ACHIEVEMENTS
**Consensus All-American, 1973**

*Height/Weight: 6-0/180    High School: St. Thomas More, Norwich, Conn.    College: Providence College, 1970-1973*

# 95 Hersey HAWKINS

## CAREER STATS

**Career Pts: 3,008**

**Scoring Avg: 24.1**

**Assists Avg: 6.5**

**Field Goal %: .539**

**TOURNAMENT PLAY**
**NCAA: 1986, 1988
(1-2)**

**NIT: 1987**

**AWARDS AND
ACHIEVEMENTS**
**Oscar Robertson
Trophy, 1988**

**Consensus
All-American, 1988**

*Born: Sept. 29, 1966, Chicago*

## "I watched Hersey play guard for about an hour and I knew he would be a four-year starter in college and a 10-year pro." —Dick Versace

There never was a question others on the 1984 Illinois all-state team would become NCAA stars: Lowell Hamilton, Ed Horton, Roger McClendon. His superb senior year at Westinghouse Vocational placed Hersey Hawkins in their company as a prep star, but not as a college prospect.

Hawkins was a 6-3 center. The horizon for a 6-3 high school center usually involves four years of majoring in pre-law at a Division III school. In the days before club basketball allowed players to escape the personnel needs and limitations of their school teams, a prospect in Hawkins' circumstance often was overlooked by college scouts.

Bradley coach Dick Versace was skeptical, but agreed to watch a Westinghouse practice arranged so that Hawkins could show his ability to function as a guard. It turned out Hawkins was positioned inside because he was needed there and not because there was nowhere else he could play. "I watched Hersey play guard for about an hour," Versace said later, "and I knew he would be a four-year starter in college and a 10-year pro."

Hawkins was in the lineup all four seasons for Bradley. He became his school's points leader and the No. 6 career scorer in NCAA Division I. He and the Braves compiled a 32-3 season in 1985-86 and a 26-5 record in 1987-88, his senior year. The toughness developed playing in the post in one of the nation's top high school leagues helped him establish a scorer's mentality as he constructed a flawlessly efficient jumper. He shot better than 50 percent in all four seasons, but only as a senior demonstrated vast range.

As a senior leading the nation in scoring with a 36.3 average, he broke Chet Walker's school record by scoring 51 points against UC Irvine. He later took out that mark and the Missouri Valley Conference record, held by Oscar Robertson, with 63 points in beating Detroit. Hawkins accumulated that total despite attempting only 28 shots; he hit 21. That game helped him to lead the nation in scoring with a 36.3 average and be named player of the year by the United States Basketball Writers Association—the honor that now bears Robertson's name.

**Height/Weight:** *6-3/195*   **High School:** *Westinghouse Vocational, Chicago*   **College:** *Bradley University, 1984-1988*

# 96 Jimmy WALKER

I t is less than an hour's drive from the Roxbury section of Boston to the city of Providence, but Jimmy Walker took the long road to get there. He traveled by way of North Carolina, or he might never have become a star guard for the Friars.

Walker came late to basketball, developing as a young teenager but owning no particular ambition to attend college. He was enrolled at Boston Trade school when he was noticed on a rec center playground by Celtics star Sam Jones. Eventually, Jones arranged for Walker to attend his prep school, Laurinburg Institute in North Carolina, which helped Walker progress as a player and establish the necessary academic credentials to gain admission to Providence.

Walker immediately became one of the great players in New England basketball. After driving his freshman squad at Providence to an unbeaten record, Walker was the leading scorer for a varsity team that won the first 19 games of his sophomore season. The Friars were 22-1 entering the 1965 NCAA Tournament and ranked No. 4 in the polls. Walker averaged 20.3 points in tournament games as Providence advanced to the East Region final, but Princeton All-American Bill Bradley demolished the Friars there with 41 points in a 109-69 Tigers triumph.

This was as close as Walker would come to the Final Four, but his own prominence only increased during the next two years. In the Holiday Festival tournament at Madison Square Garden his junior season, he averaged 39.3 points and 7.7 assists—in the title game against Boston College, he scored 50—and was named most valuable player. When Walker finished 1965-66 with an average of 24.5 points and Providence compiled a record of 22-5, coach Joe Mullaney called him the best guard he'd coached, though he'd previously worked with Lenny Wilkens and John Egan.

Walker's chief advantages over his predecessors and opponents were his size and strength. Often compared to Cincinnati's Oscar Robertson, Walker was two inches shorter but had similar power in his legs and torso and tried to adopt the same diverse approach to the game. He was as much a passer and punishing rebounder as a shooter, though he finished ahead of Lew Alcindor as a senior in 1966-67 and led the nation in scoring at 30.4 points per game. Walker had come a long, long way.

*Born: April 8, 1944, Roxbury, Mass.*

*Walker's chief advantages over his predecessors and opponents were his size and strength.*

**CAREER STATS**

Career Pts: **2,045**

Scoring Avg: **25.2**

Rebounding Avg: **6.3**

Field Goal %: **.492**

**TOURNAMENT PLAY**
**NCAA: 1965, 1966
(2-2)**

**NIT: 1967**

**AWARDS AND ACHIEVEMENTS**
**Consensus
All-American, 1967**

**Consensus
All-American, 1966**

*Height/Weight: 6-3/205    High School: Laurinburg (N.C.) Institute    College: Providence College, 1964-1967*

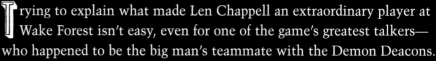

# 97 Len CHAPPELL

Trying to explain what made Len Chappell an extraordinary player at Wake Forest isn't easy, even for one of the game's greatest talkers—who happened to be the big man's teammate with the Demon Deacons.

"People used to say, 'Lenny can't do a damned thing, except rebound and score,' " said Billy Packer, who played with Chappell on Wake's 1962 Final Four team.

Chappell was a 6-8 center in a period when more at that position were approaching the 7-foot mark. He was a brawny, powerful player unafraid to use his strength inside but never more dangerous than when stepping 18 or 20 feet from the goal for an open shot. He did not entirely compensate for his height with great leaping ability, though he did jump well for a player with his stature.

"He used his body as a presence on the inside," said Packer, the regular analyst for two decades on Final Four telecasts. "He didn't just produce big numbers; he was very consistent. He'd get 30 points and 16 rebounds, but he'd do it every night."

That Chappell played center for Wake Forest did not prevent him from demonstrating flawless shooting form from nearly any range. "It was probably his most unusual attribute. He had a soft touch—with range, as well as inside," Packer said. "He was a great shooter, not a good shooter."

In the 40 years after Chappell completed his career at Wake, no player in the Atlantic Coast Conference was able to match Chappell's feat of averaging 30 points for a season.

He did not score merely in pursuit of individual glory. Chappell's efforts resulted in Wake Forest's first two ACC Tournament championships and the program's only Final Four appearance. Chappell and Packer had been recruited from opposite ends of Pennsylvania by Wake coach Bones McKinney to form the heart of what would become the school's finest team.

The Deacons recovered from a 9-8 start to win 12 consecutive games entering the national semifinals against highly regarded Ohio State. They fell, 84-68, but Chappell's last real game ended with him outscoring Buckeyes All-American Jerry Lucas by a 27-19 margin. McKinney said many times during Chappell's career he would not trade his big man for any college center, including Lucas. It was big talk, backed up by a big man.

*Born: Jan. 31, 1941, Portage, Pa.*

*"He was a great shooter, not a good shooter."*

—Billy Packer

## CAREER STATS

Career Pts: **2,165**

Scoring Avg: **24.9**

Rebounding Avg: **13.9**

Field Goal %: **.507**

**TOURNAMENT PLAY**
NCAA: 1961, 1962 (5-2)

NCAA Final Four: 1962

**AWARDS AND
ACHIEVEMENTS**
Consensus
All-American, 1962

Converse
All-American, 1961

*Height/Weight:* **6-8/240** *High School:* **Portage Area High** *College:* **Wake Forest University, 1959-1962**

# 98 Calbert CHEANEY

If Bob Knight could have designed the ideal player to transport his Indiana motion offense into the 1990s, the result of his experiment would have looked a lot like Calbert Cheaney.

While contemporaries such as Memphis' Penny Hardaway and Michigan's Chris Webber dazzled opponents and fans with fancy passes and spectacular dunks, Cheaney churned through the intricacies of Knight's attack to establish himself as the greatest scorer in Big Ten basketball.

Lacking the airborne athleticism that became essential in wing players following the Michael Jordan revolution, Cheaney was slightly overlooked as a prospect in Evansville, Ind. Even Knight wasn't impressed the first time he scouted Cheaney, but the more he watched the more he saw.

Jumping ability never was as important in Knight's program as work ethic and shooting skill. Knight considered Cheaney one of the hardest workers he coached. His shooting touch led to a career field-goal percentage that would have pleased a 7-foot center.

Cheaney did most of his work close to the ground and close to the goal. When other players were infatuated with the 3-point shot, he perfected a 14-foot corner jump shot others deemed obsolete. Of his 2,613 points, only 444 were scored on 3-point shots, though his career long-distance percentage was a remarkable .438. He was lefthanded, the first lefty to play a significant role for Knight, and that helped disarm defenders who had enough trouble countering Indiana's offensive tactics from a single direction.

In his senior season, 1992-93, Cheaney averaged 22.4 points, led Indiana to the final No. 1 poll ranking and earned consensus player of the year honors. That became the last of Knight's teams to earn a Big Ten championship. Favored to win the NCAA title, Indiana got a minimal contribution from power forward Alan Henderson, a key rebounder and defender who was injured late in the season, and lost to Kansas in the regional finals.

The Hoosiers did not end the year as the nation's No. 1 team, but they did have the No. 1 player. Cheaney was presented national player of the year awards by 13 organizations. That was spectacular enough.

*Born: July 17, 1971, Evansville, Ind.*    *Height/Weight: 6-6/210*    *High School: Harrison High, Evansville*    *College: Indiana University, 1989-1993*

*When other players were infatuated with the 3-point shot, he perfected a 14-foot corner jump shot others deemed obsolete.*

## CAREER STATS

Career Pts: **2,613**

Scoring Avg: **19.8**

Rebounding Avg: **5.4**

Field Goal %: **.559**

### TOURNAMENT PLAY
NCAA: 1990, 1991, 1992, 1993 (9-4)

NCAA Final Four: 1992

### AWARDS AND ACHIEVEMENTS
Robertson Trophy, Naismith Award, Wooden Award, 1993

Consensus All-American, 1993

# 99 Billy CUNNINGHAM

Playing under Dean Smith was not part of the deal when Billy Cunningham agreed to join the North Carolina basketball program. Frank McGuire was the coach who recruited him, a man with a national championship on his resume and a proven track record of turning New Yorkers into Tar Heels heroes.

McGuire left for the NBA before Cunningham's first UNC game, and those first few years under Smith did not produce the team success Heels players—and fans—were accustomed to enjoying. When Cunningham was a senior, following a crushing ACC loss to Wake Forest, he and some teammates happened upon a commotion outside a dormitory. They saw a figure representing Smith hung over a tree and consumed in flames. Cunningham tore it down and stamped out the fire. That was his coach.

The Tar Heels did not reach the NCAA Tournament during Cunningham's three seasons. Their composite record was 42-27. In retrospect, this was the foundation for the greatest run of uninterrupted excellence any NCAA basketball program has conceived. At the time, it felt like mediocrity.

Cunningham was one element of that period that obviously fit with the Carolina that defeated Wilt Chamberlain and Kansas for the 1957 NCAA title and the Carolina that later would yield Phil Ford, Michael Jordan and Antawn Jamison.

A 6-4 forward when he signed at Carolina, Cunningham's size seemed not to matter because of the leaping ability that earned him the "Kangaroo Kid" nickname. He grew to 6-6 and led North Carolina in scoring and rebounding in his three seasons. Wake Forest forward Frank Christie called him tougher to defend than Duke star Art Heyman and Ohio State legend Jerry Lucas.

Cunningham declined to be bound by the limits of a particular position. He passed, scored, rebounded and used that jumping ability to block shots. "Cunningham with a basketball in his hands was a man among boys," wrote Ron Green Sr. in the *Charlotte News*. "He was not a picture shooter like a Rick Barry or a David Thompson. His shots were pretty only because they were magical, usually coming at the end of some dazzling move he made up in mid-air. He was an artist on the court."

**Born: June 3, 1943, Brooklyn, N.Y.**

## Cunningham's size seemed not to matter because of the leaping ability that earned him the "Kangaroo Kid" nickname.

**CAREER STATS**

Career Pts: **1,709**    Scoring Avg: **24.8**

Rebounding Avg: **15.4**    Field Goal %: **.473**

AWARDS AND ACHIEVEMENTS: Helms Foundation All-American, 1965    U.S. Basketball Writers All-American, 1964

*Height/Weight: 6-6/210    High School: Erasmus Hall High, Brooklyn    College: University of North Carolina, 1962-1965*

# 100 Danny AINGE

ollege basketball's best third baseman understood he was 94 feet removed from never again firing a jump shot that mattered. BYU trailed Notre Dame by a basket in the 1981 NCAA Tournament round of 16, and Danny Ainge had eight seconds to change that or face the end of his playing career.

One of the most gifted natural athletes to play Division I basketball, Ainge already was a baseball major-leaguer. Though his on-court accomplishments grew daily during the 1980-81 season, he insisted he would pursue a career with the Toronto Blue Jays. His last college game would be his last game as a competitive basketball player. This was not to be the night.

Notre Dame had covered Ainge with a box-and-one defense and permitted him only nine shots. He planned to advance the ball on that last play and pass to a teammate, but Notre Dame stretched its defense to cover the entire court. "I was able to weave through the whole defense and get all the way to the rim," Ainge said. "It was one of the few open looks I got."

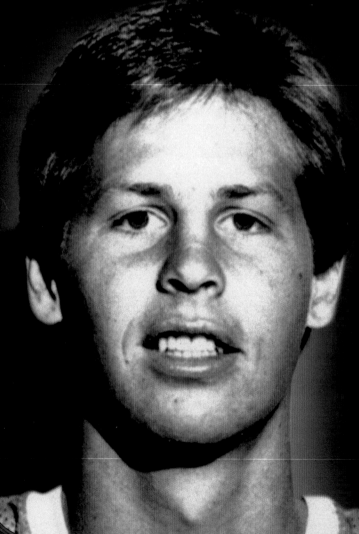

Ainge's end-to-end drive for that game-winning layup ranks among the most famous NCAA Tournament plays. That raised the profile of a player whose excellence was not widely recognized because he played in the Western Athletic Conference.

Growing up in Oregon, he'd been smitten with the glamour of the Pacific-8. But his recruiting visit to BYU convinced him he belonged on a campus whose students embraced the values of the Mormon Church. Ainge instantly became one of the top college guards. He averaged 21.1 points and 5.3 assists as a freshman. He ran the offense and was the offense. His scoring average never dipped below 18.4, and he never shot lower than 52 percent. He set an NCAA record by scoring in double figures in 111 consecutive games.

Though he believed in his baseball ability, he recognized something special about his time on the court. "As my college career went on," Ainge said. "I just recognized that basketball was in my blood." He retired from baseball and became an NBA champion as a Boston Celtics guard. There was plenty of basketball left in him.

**Born: March 17, 1959, Eugene, Ore.**

> *"As my college career went on, I just recognized that basketball was in my blood."*
>
> —Danny Ainge

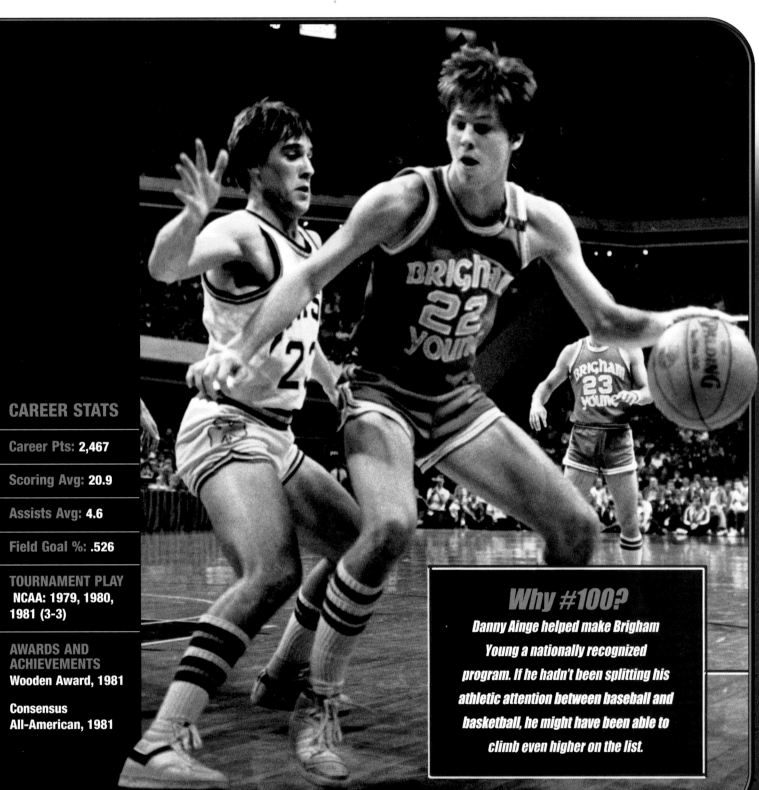

## CAREER STATS

**Career Pts: 2,467**

**Scoring Avg: 20.9**

**Assists Avg: 4.6**

**Field Goal %: .526**

### TOURNAMENT PLAY
NCAA: 1979, 1980, 1981 (3-3)

### AWARDS AND ACHIEVEMENTS
Wooden Award, 1981

Consensus All-American, 1981

### Why #100?
Danny Ainge helped make Brigham Young a nationally recognized program. If he hadn't been splitting his athletic attention between baseball and basketball, he might have been able to climb even higher on the list.

Height/Weight: 6-5/175   High School: North Eugene High   College: Brigham Young University, 1977-1981

# INDEX

| Name | College | Years | Rank | Page No. |
|------|---------|-------|------|----------|
| Kurland, Bob | Oklahoma A&M | 1942-46 | 27 | 64 |
| Laettner, Christian | Duke | 1988-92 | 9 | 28 |
| Lamar, Bo | Southwestern Louisiana | 1971-73 | 81 | 153 |
| Lanier, Bob | St. Bonaventure | 1967-70 | 34 | 76 |
| Lee, Butch | Marquette | 1974-78 | 50 | 100 |
| Lee, Keith | Memphis State | 1981-85 | 72 | 138 |
| Lovellette, Clyde | Kansas | 1949-52 | 42 | 90 |
| Lucas, Jerry | Ohio State | 1959-62 | 10 | 30 |
| Lucas, John | Maryland | 1972-76 | 90 | 168 |
| Luisetti, Hank | Stanford | 1935-38 | 46 | 96 |
| Manning, Danny | Kansas | 1984-88 | 12 | 34 |
| Maravich, Pete | LSU | 1967-70 | 5 | 20 |
| Martin, Kenyon | Cincinnati | 1996-00 | 91 | 170 |
| May, Scott | Indiana | 1973-76 | 32 | 74 |
| McDaniels, Jim | Western Kentucky | 1968-71 | 73 | 140 |
| Meminger, Dean | Marquette | 1968-72 | 93 | 174 |
| Mikan, George | DePaul | 1942-46 | 20 | 50 |
| Moncrief, Sidney | Arkansas | 1975-79 | 76 | 146 |
| Mount, Rick | Purdue | 1967-70 | 23 | 56 |
| Mullin, Chris | St. John's | 1981-85 | 30 | 70 |
| Murphy, Calvin | Niagara | 1967-70 | 47 | 97 |
| Olajuwon, Akeem | Houston | 1981-84 | 53 | 106 |
| O'Neal, Shaquille | LSU | 1989-92 | 66 | 126 |
| Pettit, Bob | LSU | 1951-54 | 36 | 80 |
| Robertson, Oscar | Cincinnati | 1957-60 | 3 | 16 |
| Robinson, David | Navy | 1983-87 | 74 | 142 |
| Robinson, Glenn | Purdue | 1992-94 | 62 | 120 |
| Rodgers, Guy | Temple | 1955-58 | 82 | 154 |
| Rosenbluth, Lennie | North Carolina | 1954-57 | 61 | 118 |
| Russell, Bill | San Francisco | 1953-56 | 4 | 18 |
| Russell, Cazzie | Michigan | 1961-66 | 25 | 60 |
| Sampson, Ralph | Virginia | 1979-83 | 39 | 86 |
| Simmons, Lionel | LaSalle | 1986-90 | 79 | 150 |
| Thomas, Isiah | Indiana | 1979-81 | 18 | 46 |
| Thompson, David | N.C. State | 1972-75 | 6 | 22 |
| Tisdale, Wayman | Oklahoma | 1982-85 | 52 | 104 |
| Unseld, Wes | Louisville | 1965-68 | 58 | 116 |
| Walker, Chet | Bradley | 1959-62 | 84 | 157 |
| Walker, Jimmy | Providence | 1964-67 | 96 | 180 |
| Walton, Bill | UCLA | 1971-74 | 2 | 14 |
| West, Jerry | West Virginia | 1957-60 | 13 | 36 |
| Wicks, Sidney | UCLA | 1973-76 | 33 | 75 |
| Williams, Jason | Duke | 1999-02 | 37 | 82 |
| Williamson, Corliss | Arkansas | 1992-99 | 88 | 164 |
| Wooden, John | Purdue | 1929-32 | 58 | 114 |
| Worthy, James | North Carolina | 1979-82 | 57 | 112 |